Digital Media as Ambient Therapy

Digital Media as Ambient Therapy explores the ways "mental illness" can emerge from our relationships (with ourselves, others, and the world), to address the concern around what kind of relationality is conducive for "mental health" and what role digital technologies can play in fostering such relationality.

Exploring the rise of ambient—that is to say, ubiquitous, surrounding, and environmental—technologies and their impact on our understanding of "mental health," sanity, and therapy, this book critically examines the work of influential contemporary social theorists such as Hartmut Rosa and investigates case studies that reveal new modes of digitally mediated intimacy and attention, such as ASMR and QAnon. It also poses the question of what "mental health" and "mental illness" mean for subjects increasingly faced with a maddening sense of interconnectedness.

This book offers new perspectives for academics and postgraduates interested in critical discussions of alienation, digital technology, and contemporary social theory.

Francis Russell is an independent researcher and a trade union official based in Boorloo (Perth), Western Australia. He worked as a lecturer in cultural studies for over a decade, and is one of the founders of the School of Critical Arts, an independent organisation for the study of philosophy and contemporary art. He is the author of numerous peer-reviewed articles on the relationship between alienation, "mental illness," and neoliberalism. Along with artist David Attwood he co-edited the book *The Art of Laziness: Contemporary Art and Post-Work Politics*.

Routledge Studies in New Media and Cyberculture

56 Digital Ageism
How it Operates and Approaches to Tackling it
Andrea Rosales, Mireia Fernández-Ardèvol & Jakob Svensson

57 Queer Reflections on AI
Uncertain Intelligences
Michael Klipphahn-Karge, Ann-Kathrin Koster & Sara Morais dos Santos Bruss

58 Pandemics in the Age of Social Media
Information and Misinformation in Developing Nations
Edited by Vikas Kumar and Mohit Rewari

59 The Chinese Internet: Political Economy and Digital Discourse
Yuqi Na

60 Mapping Lies in the Global Media Sphere
Tirşe Filibeli & Melis Öneren Özbek

61 Digital Media as Ambient Therapy
The Ecological Self between Resonance and Alienation
Francis Russell

Digital Media as Ambient Therapy

The Ecological Self between Resonance and Alienation

Francis Russell

LONDON AND NEW YORK

First published 2024
by Routledge
4 Park Square, Milton Park, Abingdon, Oxon OX14 4RN

and by Routledge
605 Third Avenue, New York, NY 10158

Routledge is an imprint of the Taylor & Francis Group, an informa business

© 2024 Francis Russell

The right of Francis Russell to be identified as author of this work has been asserted in accordance with sections 77 and 78 of the Copyright, Designs and Patents Act 1988.

All rights reserved. No part of this book may be reprinted or reproduced or utilised in any form or by any electronic, mechanical, or other means, now known or hereafter invented, including photocopying and recording, or in any information storage or retrieval system, without permission in writing from the publishers.

Trademark notice: Product or corporate names may be trademarks or registered trademarks, and are used only for identification and explanation without intent to infringe.

British Library Cataloguing-in-Publication Data
A catalogue record for this book is available from the British Library

Library of Congress Cataloging-in-Publication Data
Names: Russell, Francis (Researcher), author.
Title: Digital media as ambient therapy: the ecological self between resonance and alienation / Francis Russell.
Description: Abingdon, Oxon; New York, NY: Routledge, 2024. | Series: Routledge studies in new media and cyberculture | Includes bibliographical references and index.
Identifiers: LCCN 2023055876 (print) | LCCN 2023055877 (ebook) | ISBN 9781032101347 (hardback) | ISBN 9781032104119 (paperback) | ISBN 9781003215202 (ebook)
Subjects: LCSH: Mental illness in mass media. | Digital media–Social aspects. | Digital media–Psychological aspects. | Alienation (Social psychology)
Classification: LCC P96.M45 R87 2024 (print) | LCC P96.M45 (ebook) | DDC 362.2–dc23/eng/20240108
LC record available at https://lccn.loc.gov/2023055876
LC ebook record available at https://lccn.loc.gov/2023055877

ISBN: 978-1-032-10134-7 (hbk)
ISBN: 978-1-032-10411-9 (pbk)
ISBN: 978-1-003-21520-2 (ebk)

DOI: 10.4324/9781003215202

Typeset in Times New Roman
by Deanta Global Publishing Services, Chennai, India

Contents

Acknowledgements   *vi*

Introduction   1

1   From "Mental Illness" to "Environmental Illness"   11

2   Mute Instruments and Resonant Relations   33

3   The Agonies of Freedom and Control   55

4   QAnon: From the Resonant to the Digitally Sublime   78

Conclusion   102

Index   *107*

Acknowledgements

This book emerged out of the COVID-19 pandemic and the chaos and ensuing devastation that resounded throughout the Australian higher education sector. Given the challenges caused by COVID-19, and the urgent demands made by the industrial campaigns run by the National Tertiary Education Union (NTEU) during this time—some of which I proudly led at Curtin University—I was convinced at various moments during this book's development that I would be unable to complete it.

As such, thanks must be given to the numerous people without whom this book would not have been possible. Thank you to Katie Ellis for supporting this project from its earliest moments; to Mad Magladry who helped me conceive of the book's scope in its initial stages; to Robert Briggs and Matthew Chrulew for helping me to think beyond many of my conceptual dead ends; and to Ben Rich and Eva Bujalka for their consistent encouragement.

A note of appreciation must also be given to all of my comrades in the NTEU, as our collective struggles helped to remind me that academic inquiry is worth defending. In particular, Scott Fitzgerald and Wayne Cupido must be thanked for reminding me that critical thought must, and does, happen every day.

Lastly, thanks to Amy Hickman, for everything.

Introduction

In the wake of the COVID-19 pandemic, there has been increased discussion on the necessity of utilising advancements in digital technology to meet the explosion of demand for therapeutic responses to common "mental illnesses" such as anxiety and depression. As the World Health Organization reported, in March 2022, not only that there is evidence to suggest that the global pandemic resulted in "a worldwide increase in "mental health" problems, including widespread depression and anxiety," but that the pandemic also "further widened the "mental health" treatment gap, [as] outpatient "mental health" services have been particularly disrupted" (WHO 2022, 6). While an increased emphasis on digital technology in "mental healthcare" was noticeable prior to the pandemic—as evinced by reports such as the UK National Health Service's "The Digital Future of Mental Healthcare and its Workforce" (Foley and Woollard 2019)—the pandemic saw speculations around digital "mental healthcare" turn into overnight realities. As "mental health" not-for-profits such as Australia's Black Dog Institute argued, the increased demand for "mental health" services alongside the risks posed by face-to-face interactions increased the need for governments to invest in "technology-enabled "mental health" services such as mobile apps, telehealth, and online treatment" (2020).

Beyond highlighting the increasingly digital character of "mental healthcare," the pandemic's lockdowns and self-isolation requirements also raised the question of the ecological character of therapeutic practice. By ecological, I don't mean only to refer to the natural world and the human being's relationship to it. Of course, the impact of deforestation, the treatment of livestock, and the impacts of global trade and transport on the non-human world were all openly discussed as precipitating factors in the development and spread of the novel coronavirus and the ensuing lockdowns. Furthermore, questions of urban air pollution, and discussions of a desire to escape the temporality of city life and to return to the country via remote working, were also common features of pandemic discourse. Nevertheless, it is also important to attend to what could be called, following Eric Hörl, the question of the relationship between "mental health" and denaturalised ecologies. Hörl draws our attention to the manifold of ecologies that proliferate today: "ecologies of

DOI: 10.4324/9781003215202-1

sensation, perception, cognition, desire, attention, power, values, information, participation, media, the mind, relations, practices, behaviour, belonging, the social, the political—to name only a selection of possible examples" (2017, 1). Indeed, such is the extent of the denaturalisation of ecology that, for Hörl, the term refers neither to the non-technological nor to the "dogmas of proximity and immediacy; of the familiar and of kinship; of the healthy and the unscathed; of the proper, the house, etc." (2017, 1). Instead, ecology today refers to

> the collaboration of a multiplicity of human and nonhuman agents: it is something like the cipher of a new thinking of togetherness and of a great cooperation of entities and forces, which has begun to be significant for contemporary thought; hence it forces and drives a radically relational onto-epistemological renewal.
>
> (2017, 3)

Similarly, the event of the Anthropocene has rendered almost unthinkable the notion of a natural environment that is unmediated by technology. While we continue to characterise environments as urban or rural, as tranquil or stressful, as beautiful or desolate, such distinctions occur alongside a general confluence of the human and non-human, and of the organic and inorganic. Accordingly, to say that COVID-19 helped to underline the question of the ecological character of "mental illnesses" is to underline that "mental illnesses" were being increasingly discussed in terms of relationality and mediation—and, more specifically, digital mediation.

Of course, discussion of the social causes of "mental illness" and the relationship between "mental health" and technology have been ongoing throughout the twentieth century. Mid-twentieth-century psychiatrists, sociologists, and philosophers such as R.D. Laing (2010 [1960]), Thomas Szasz (2011 [1961]), Erving Goffman (2022 [1961]), and Michel Foucault (2009 [1961]) helped to popularise questions around the institutional formation of what are (now) called "mental illnesses." Through the works of such figures, academic and general audiences were provoked to wrestle with "mental illnesses" as something other than individual moral or biological failings, and instead as subject positions that were socially and politically formed through institutions like the asylum and family. Similarly, there is a long history of attempts to explain "mental illness" by way of changes to the technological modes of communication in society. As Jeffrey Sconce has pointed out, it was common in the mid-twentieth century to find critiques of television constructed—especially by media critics suspicious of mass culture—on the grounds that it encouraged delusional or even psychotic states in viewers (2019, 2). Similarly, and as Amy Orben has recounted, paediatricians like Mary Preston published works in the early 1940s suggesting radio crime dramas were leading hundreds of children to develop nervous conditions (2020, 1143). Nevertheless, given the enthusiasm for neurobiological accounts of "mental illnesses" and psychopharmacological approaches to "mental healthcare" that has reigned at least since the 1990s (see Chapter 1), COVID-19 helped to usher in a renewed interest in discussions of the social and technological factors precipitating "mental illnesses." The two most obvious examples of this are the impacts of lockdowns and isolation on rates of depression, anxiety, and suicidality, and a corresponding concern over the effect that digital platforms have on these phenomena. In news media, concerns have been raised over the increased time spent on applications such as TikTok during the isolation and boredom of lockdowns (Paul 2022). Psychiatrists have pointed to the spread of misinformation regarding neurological disorders such as ADHD on TikTok, and have raised concerns that the application is accelerating rates of misdiagnosis and inappropriate self-diagnosis (Yeung et al. 2022). In a similar vein, media scholars have studied the phenomenon of lockdown "doom scrolling"—the act of compulsively following negative news stories via one's smartphone and social media feeds—and its impact on "mental health" (Ytre-Arne and Moe 2021).[1]

Shared by all of these academic and popular accounts is a concern for the way the pandemic has helped to render legible certain ecological changes—or, put differently, changes to our digitally mediated relationality—that are transforming "mental illnesses" and that supposedly require the adoption of new digitally mediated forms of "mental healthcare." In response to such a concern, this book explores competing theorisations of the impacts of digital media on the conceptualisation and treatment of "mental illnesses," and critically assesses recent attempts to theorise non-pathological modes of relationality, as can be found in the influential work of sociologist Hartmut Rosa. Put differently, this book engages with the problem of whether relationality—which is today increasingly thought in terms of ecology—can be understood in pathological and non-pathological forms. Is the ever-expanding digital mediation of the social world exacerbating "mental illnesses," such that we must think through strategies for reshaping sociality and discovering new "healthy" modes of togetherness? And, if so, what exactly is missing or marginalised in today's social world? Is it something somatic, like touch? something political, like solidarity? something temporal, like deceleration? or something hermeneutic, like meaning? In order to grapple with these questions, this book explores competing theorisations of the impacts of digital media on the conceptualisation and treatment of "mental illnesses," and, in particular, in digital media *qua* the notion of ambient media, and "mental illness" *qua* the notion of environmental illness.

"Mental Illness" and Environmental Illness

A question that the reader has most likely held throughout the first part of this introduction is why the terms "mental illness," "mental health," and "mental healthcare" have been rhetorically distanced through the use of quotation marks. The very notion of "mental illness" is hotly contested within psychiatry and psychology—let alone within psychoanalytic, Marxist, feminist, queer, and anti-colonial discourses that seek to disrupt hegemonic forms of psychiatric knowledge and power. Neither the mental nor the pathological components of the compound noun "mental illness" are assured. On the one hand, the "mental" half can risk overshadowing the corporeal, social, political, technological, and extra-cerebral but biological aspects of "mental illnesses." On the other hand, the "illness" half can privilege medical knowledge over other practices of healing, just as it can reinforce hegemonic notions of normality and the stigmatisation of social differences.

For this reason, a growing movement both inside and outside of the academy is reappropriating the term madness in order to further the demedicalisation and depsychologisation of emotional and behavioural difference. As Richard A. Ingram has noted in his *A Genealogy of the Concept of "Mad Studies"*, the academic discipline of mad studies emerged out of the largely North American—specifically Canadian—mad movements and mad pride events (Ingram 2022, 93–94). Ingram points to having read activist and educator Irit Shimrat's 1997 book *Call Me Crazy: Stories from the Mad Movement* as helping him to solidify a counterhegemonic notion of madness (2022, 93). While mad studies, and the various mad movements across the world, cannot be subsumed under a single logic or framework, the introduction of Shimrat's book provides a pithy and provocative insight into a shared sentiment in mad studies. She writes:

> *Call Me Crazy* is about people who have done an unusual thing: we stopped being mental patients. That's not supposed to happen, since "mental illness" is supposed to be an incurable biological disease. Certainly you're not supposed to reject the idea that you're sick, stop taking your medications, refuse to ever see a psychiatrist again, join with others in questioning psychiatry and get a life as a result. That would mean they were wrong about you. That might mean they're wrong about a lot of people.
>
> (1997, 1)

It is worth emphasising that Shimrat's views here on psychiatry and psychopharmacology are not synonymous with mad studies *tout court*. Nevertheless, the rejection of biologisitic accounts of "mental illness," and a rejection of a psychiatric monopoly over the truths and knowledges that pertain to madness, is a key feature of almost all mad studies discourse. Similar to, and in many cases explicitly drawing on, the social model of disability and the affirmative model of disability (Swain and French 2000), mad studies attempt to think through the difference between various institutional models of "mental illness," and madness as a form of difference that is untragic and that can be embraced. As Ingram states, referring to a manifesto he authored in 2008:

> we await the time when our epiphanies are no longer misrecognized as mania or psychosis; when our dry spells are no longer misrecognized as depression; when our frenetic energies are no longer misrecognized as ADHD or borderline personality disorder; and when our search for an inner place of refuge is no longer recognized as autism.
> (2022, 95)

Given the powerful conceptual resources provided by mad studies, one could ask why the clumsier use of "mental illness" has been embraced over the potentially more radical and elegant term madness. There are two reasons for this choice. Firstly, this book is not a work of mad studies, and the adoption of "mental illness" has been specifically chosen to make clear that this text does not privilege the experience and knowledge of those who identify as mad, or are involved in the discipline of mad studies or the mad movements. This text is largely a work of theory, and one that stakes its intervention at the level of the competing theoretical approaches to understanding the relationship between digital media and "mental illness." Put differently, it is out of respect to what is unique about mad studies as a discipline, and also out of a desire to be clear about the methodological approach adopted in this text, that the term madness has not been used. Secondly, the term "mental illness" and related terms such as "mental health" and "mental healthcare" are useful insofar as they signal that this book is concerned with broad shifts within neoliberal societies rather than within important, but unfortunately, marginal academic and activist institutions and discourses. For the vast majority of people, the term "mental illness" still has a great deal of purchase, even if it is unclear as to what extent the public is committed to a biological or medical model of "mental illness."[2] However, in order to avoid any endorsement of such medical and biological approaches, this book retains the use of quotation marks when deploying the term "mental illness." In this way, the use of "mental illness" is somewhat like Jacques Derrida's textual strategy of placing concepts *sous rature* or "under erasure" (1997, 60). To place a concept under erasure is to acknowledge that, within a certain context, a concept might be unavoidable or necessary even if it is problematic or untenable.

However, this book does not limit itself to a discussion of "mental illness" alone, but outlines recent transformations of this concept. As will be discussed further in the next section, a key object of inquiry for this book is the emergence of new and relational accounts of "mental illness" in neoliberal societies. As I will discuss in detail in Chapter 1, the emergence of what I call environmental illness can be traced back to the ecological thought described by figures like Hörl. To understand "mental illnesses" as environmental illnesses is not just to understand "mental illness" as arising from a context, and involving intersubjective relationships, but is also to acknowledge that painful experiences referred to as depression, anxiety, and psychosis—for example—are themselves co-produced by complex relationships between the human and nonhuman world, and with the latter encompassing both the organic and inorganic.

Ambient Media

As discussed at the beginning of this introduction, the shift towards digitally mediated forms of "mental healthcare" looks to be accelerating as a result of the COVID-19 pandemic. However, it is important to acknowledge that this acceleration is occurring within a period of intense media saturation, and this saturation, or this state of being surrounded by media, is signalled in this book with the phrase *ambient media*. As the media theorist Ulrik Schmidt notes, when approached as an aesthetic experience, something is ambient insofar as it produces the "distinctive *effect* characterised by an *intensification of the experience of being surrounded*" (2013, 176). As such, ambience "can be described as the experience that a phenomenon 'goes around' the subject" (2013, 176). For my purposes, ambience is useful insofar as the term alerts us to a new mediated condition in which digital technologies are increasingly experienced as a field or an environment in which one finds oneself—that is to say, that one becomes increasingly surrounded by media rather than encountering them in discrete settings—and in which advanced forms of digital media gain their instrumental value through their capacity to give the individual user the sense of being placed at the centre of something, or of being surrounded. For Schmidt, ambient experiences have become increasingly central to media culture since at least the 1960s, insofar as:

> the emergence of new strategic paradigms for everyday human-centric computing environments such as *ubiquitous computing* (ubicomp) and *ambient intelligence* as well as the digital distributions of information as what has been called "ambient informatics" have strengthened the tendency to move toward ambient aestheticization of digital media and information tools.
>
> (2013, 176)

While I will go into more detail in the next chapter, ambient media can refer to specialised media that invite a specific aesthetic experience—such as the ambient music of Brian Eno or Tim Hecker—but also includes more ubiquitous kinds of media such as portable media players, smartphones, and wearable technologies. Arguably, even media artefacts of earlier periods, such as speakers and television screens, have become part of an ambiently mediated condition, insofar as forms of wireless accessibility and data storage and sharing have allowed for complex relations between media devices.

As such, this emphasis on relationality produces something of a homology between the aforementioned logic of ecology discussed by Hörl, and the logic of ambience described by Schmidt. As Schmidt puts it, ambience concerns "the complex and subtle ways different things are related in space and the discreet emotions and affections produced in the experience of such relations" (Schmidt 2013, 175). However, if ambient and ecological logics are fundamentally relational they should nevertheless be distinguished at the level of experience and perspective. Drawing on Schmidt, we can argue that ambience implies an aesthetic experience of centrality, of being surrounded, and that this is potentially missing from, or is at least not commonly associated with, conceptualisations of the ecological. Hence, while it might be tempting to treat the ambient and ecological as, if not synonymous then at least expressing similar logics, to avoid confusion and oversimplification I reserve the term ambient to refer to a media condition and its related subjectivity. As such, I distinguish the broader ecological logic described by Hörl—which can be seen underpinning a range of phenomena, such as "mental illness," for example—from the concrete example of ambient media. While a term like ambience could be used to refer to a broader logic that underpins a range of technical, cultural, and political phenomena, in the context of this book I limit the terms ambient and ambience to refer to digital media in their state of being underpinned by the ecological logic described by Hörl, and without such media being entirely subsumed by and therefore explainable through a sole appeal to such a logic.

More specifically, in the following chapters I will attempt to understand both how ambient approaches to media and ecological approaches to "mental illness" are transforming the demands made on contemporary subjects, and how these transformations reverberate through contemporary social and media theory. Not only have changes to media and changes to the conceptualisation of "mental illness" raised critical questions around the potential loss of earlier modes of subjectivity—especially those associated with humanistic values like freedom—they have also provoked speculations about new and emancipatory notions of self and other. In order to critically assess these transformations in the technological and theoretical framing of "mental illness," Chapter 1 elaborates on the discussion of ambient media and environmental illness provided in this introduction. This chapter explores the decline of biologistic accounts of "mental illness" and the renewed and expansive discussion of relationality in the context of "mental healthcare." In doing so, I provide a broad overview of environmental illness and ambient therapeutic media by exploring changes in digital technology and psychiatric discourse. Chapter 2 provides a more robust theoretical account of the relational character of environmental illness by producing a new reading of Hartmut Rosa's *Resonance*. While this latter text is not explicitly concerned with "mental illness," I will attempt to construct a broader theory of environmental illness from Rosa's attempt to outline a non-metaphysical account of alienation, and its opposite, in the form of what he calls *resonance*. Through Rosa's theory of resonance and alienation, we will explore the notion that environmental illness can be understood as an alienated mode of relationality and is accordingly irreducible to simplistic biological or sociological explanations. This chapter culminates in a discussion of Rosa's concern that what I call ambient media may in fact exacerbate rather than ameliorate environmental illnesses. The third chapter turns to contemporary media theorists like Paul Roquet, Mac Hagood, and Jacinthe Flore to expand but also challenge these concerns. By linking the rise of ambient media to issues around risk and alienation within precarious neoliberal societies, this chapter outlines the arguments for viewing ambient media as a precipitating factor in the rise of environmental illnesses. In doing so, the chapter questions the notion that it is possible or desirable to affirm a "healthy" or "unalienated" notion of relationality that supposedly exists outside of an ambient media condition. The fourth chapter analyses the conspiracy theory culture of QAnon in order to explore the issues raised in the first three chapters. By interrogating the ways in which millions of people have drawn on ambient media in the attempt to overcome experiences of alienation, albeit in ways that have produced violence and political turmoil, this chapter seeks to problematise unalienated relationality—especially as theorised by Rosa—as a principle on the basis of which we can aspire to a healthier sense of self and other as mediated by digital technology.

Notes

1 Perhaps the most alarming piece of research of this kind is Kirsten R. Müller-Vahl et al.'s study of the "mass sociogenic illnesses" produced through YouTube and TikTok (2022). According to Müller-Vahl and her co-authors, during the pandemic, Tourette syndrome clinics the world over were inundated with children experiencing movements and vocalisations that were thought to be tics (2022, 477). Tourette syndrome specialists found that, not only did these tics sit outside of the range of movements and vocalisations that are expected in typical sufferers, but they also closely resembled the tics and vocalisations of popular YouTubers such as the German Jan Zimmerman (2022, 477). Moreover, Müller-Vahl and her co-authors found that a considerable number of these patients reported being "unable to perform unpleasant tasks because of their symptoms resulting in release from obligations at school and home, while symptoms temporarily completely disappear while conducting favourite activities" (2022, 477). Speculating on the causes of this explosion of Tourette-like symptoms, Müller-Vahl and her co-authors suggest that the rise of climate change anxiety or eco-anxiety amongst Generation Z, coupled with the stress, loneliness, and boredom of the pandemic lockdowns may have resulted in a kind of "culture-bound stress reaction" (2022, 478). We will return to the discussion of eco-anxiety in Chapter 1.
2 An anecdote from psychologist Richard Bentall's book *Doctoring the Mind: Why Psychiatric Treatments Fail* is useful on this point. Towards the end of the book, Bentall recounts a conversation about "mental illness" with a cab driver in

Manchester, in which the driver admits to suffering from a period of "mental illness" after the death of his wife and using antidepressant medication in response (2010, 262–64). Asking the cab driver whether the antidepressants helped, Bentall receives the somewhat ambivalent response "maybe. Dunno" (2010, 264). Rather than view this response as evasive, it is arguably a useful insight into the ambivalent relationship most have to terms like "mental illness" and to treatments like psychopharmacology. For that reason, it is unwise to assume that the common use of a term like "mental illness" implies a commitment to a particular ontological account, nor that the willingness to utilise a particular treatment implies an understanding of exactly what is being treated. Indeed, it is precisely such mutable and ambivalent understandings of "mental illness," rather than a "correct" account, that occupies this book.

References

Bentall, Richard P. 2010. *Doctoring the Mind: Why Psychiatric Treatments Fail*. London: Penguin.

Black Dog Institute. 2020. *Mental Health Ramifications of COVID-19: The Australian Context*. https://www.blackdoginstitute.org.au/wp-content/uploads/2020/04/20200319_covid19-evidence-and-reccomendations.pdf

Derrida, Jacques. 1997. *Of Grammatology*. Trans. Gayatri Chakravorty Spivak. Baltimore: John Hopkins University Press.

Foley, Tom, and Woollard, James. 2019. *The Digital Future of Mental Healthcare and Its Workforce: A Report on a Mental Health Stakeholder Engagement to Inform the Topol Review*. National Health Service. https://topol.hee.nhs.uk/downloads/digital-future-of-mental-healthcare-report/

Foucault, Michel. 2009. *History of Madness*. Trans. Jonathan Murphy and Jean Khalfa. London: Routledge.

Goffman, Erving. 2022. *Asylums: Essays on the Social Situation of Mental Patients and Other Inmates*. London: Penguin.

Hörl, Erich. 2017. "Introduction to General Ecology: The Ecologization of Thinking". In *General Ecology: The New Ecological Paradigm*. Eds. Erich Hörl with James Burton. London: Bloomsbury. 1–76.

Ingram, Richard. 2021. "A Genealogy of the Concept of Mad Studies". In *The Routledge International Handbook of Mad Studies*. Eds. Peter Beresford and Jasna Russo. London: Routledge. 93–97.

Laing, R.D. 2010. *The Divided Self: An Existential Study in Sanity and Madness*. London: Penguin.

Müller-Vahl, Kirsten R., et al. 2022. "Stop that! It's Not Tourette's But a New Type of Mass Sociogenic Illness". *Brain* 145.2: 476–480.

Orben, Amy. 2020. "The Sisyphean Cycle of Technological Panics". *Perspectives on Psychological Science* 15.5: 1143–1157.

Paul, Kari. 2022. "What TikTok Does to Your Mental Health: 'It's Embarrassing We Know So Little'". *The Guardian*, 30 October. https://www.theguardian.com/technology/2022/oct/30/tiktok-mental-health-social-media

Schmidt, Ulrich. 2013. "Ambience and Ubiquity". In *Throughout: Art and Culture Emerging with Ubiquitous Computing*. Ed. Ulrich Ekman. Cambridge, MA: MIT Press. 175–188.

Sconce, Jeffrey. 2019. *The Technical Delusion: Electronics, Power, Insanity*. Durham: Duke University Press.
Shirmat, Irit. 1997. *Call Me Crazy: Stories from the Mad Movement*. Vancouver: Press Gang Publishers.
Swain, John, and French, Sally. 2000. "Towards an Affirmative Model of Disability". *Disability & Society* 15.4: 569–582.
Szasz, Thomas. 2011. *The Myth of Mental Illness: Foundations of a Theory of Personal Conduct*. New York: Harper Perennial.
World Health Organization. 2022. *Mental Health and COVID-19: Early Evidence of the Pandemic's Impact, Scientific Brief*, 2 March. https://www.who.int/publications/i/item/WHO-2019-nCoV-Sci_Brief-Mental_health-2022.1
Yeung, Anthony, et al. 2022. "TikTok and Attention-Deficit/Hyperactivity Disorder: A Cross-Sectional Study of Social Media Content Quality". *The Canadian Journal of Psychiatry* 67.12: 881–938.
Ytre-Arne, Brita, and Moe, Hallvard. 2021. "Doomscrolling, Monitoring and Avoiding: News Use in COVID-19 Pandemic Lockdown". *Journalism Studies* 13: 1739–1755.

1 From "Mental Illness" to "Environmental Illness"

Recent decades have seen an increased interest in bringing "mental illness" out in the open. Such an interest stands against the now-marginalised understanding that "mental illness" is private—relating to one's childhood and familial relationships; intimate—discussed on the psychoanalyst's couch; and secret—both in the sense that "mental illness" was once predominantly understood to relate to the individual's deepest fantasies, fears, and the dynamics of one's unconscious mind, and in the sense of the secrets of the mental hospital or asylum that were, for many decades, disastrously excluded from public scrutiny. While it is true that anti-stigma and public awareness campaigns have done much to bring "mental illness" out in the open—as both a topic of everyday discussion, and as a purportedly normal experience, one that is part of the progression of most people's lives—broader technological, social, and political shifts have seen the profound relocation of both "mental illness" and its concomitant therapeutic practices. Indeed, whereas Deleuze and Guattari's claim that "a schizophrenic out for a walk is a better model than a neurotic lying on an analyst's couch" (2009, 2) may have once been received as a provocative refutation of psychoanalytic orthodoxy, now such a statement seems increasingly banal, insofar as "mental illness" and its treatments today appear open, ambient, atmospheric—and, as we will see in the case of wearables, ambulatory. The discourse of "mental health" circumscribes an ever-expanding field of experiences, activities, and knowledges, such that our bodies, diets, forms of exercise, forms of work, personal relationships, relationships to plants and animals, relationships to architecture, and relationships to digital media—with the latter flowing through the rest—are viewed as potential sites of the emergence of and treatment of "mental illness." "A breath of fresh air, a relationship with the outside world" (2009, 2); today, this statement could just as easily refer to the experience of "mental illness" as to its treatment.

In this chapter, I provide an overview of ambient media and ambient-mediated therapies, and the impacts both have had on our understanding and treatment of "mental illnesses." In the first section, I provide an overview of the ongoing reconceptualisation of "mental illnesses" from individual or familial pathologies into environmental illnesses. In this transition, the

DOI: 10.4324/9781003215202-2

individual's environment, and their capacity to effectively negotiate such an environment, are granted greater significance in our understanding of "mental illness." In the second section, I review theoretical accounts of ambient media and attempt to distinguish this category from more established approaches to mass media and digital technology. In doing so, I explore the ways in which such media offer new forms of intimacy and attention, thereby precipitating new and ambient modes of subjectivity. This review then facilitates, in the third section, a consideration of how ambient approaches to "mental illness," and the development of ambient media, have allowed for new approaches to treatment. To conclude, I turn to questions of governance and subjectivity, the relationship between ambient notions of media and "mental illness," and the regime of neoliberal biopolitics.

Ambient Suffering

While George Bush declared the 1990s as "the decade of the brain," the last two decades have seen a desire within psychiatry, psychology, and "mental health" advocacy to return the brain to the human being, and the human being to its environment. In terms of the latter, we are here referring to the recent acknowledgement that the neurological study of "mental illness" cannot forego a detailed understanding of human societies and the ecosystems that support them. Perhaps the greatest motivator for this turn has been the failure of neuroscience and genomics to provide increased standards of living and life expectancy for those suffering with "mental illnesses." As former director of the American National Institute for Mental Health (NIMH), Thomas Insel, has admitted that while recent decades have seen major advances in the neurological and genetic understanding of "mental illnesses," such scientific discoveries have not translated into better outcomes for those who suffer (2022). As Insel recounts, at a 2015 public event for "mental health" advocacy the former NIMH director was confronted by an angry parent whose child had been living with schizophrenia, and who was unimpressed with Insel's lecture on brain research and "mental illness" (2022, xvi). The parent's introjection, "our house is on fire and you are talking about the chemistry of the paint," provoked Insel to acknowledge that, with regards to neuroscientific research:

> nothing my colleagues and I were doing addressed the ever-increasing urgency and magnitude of the suffering millions of Americans were living through—and dying of.
>
> (Insel 2022, xvii)

Indeed, the absence of clear biomarkers for "mental illnesses," and the increasing levels of death, disability, and homelessness experienced by those deemed seriously "mentally ill" has raised questions around the efficacy of neurobiological approaches. As such, a wave of critiques has emerged demanding that psychiatry return the brain to the world. While such critiques differ in important ways, they generally share a concern that the neuroscientific approach to "mental illness" has treated the brain as an enclosed system, and has thereby obscured the social and environmental determinates of suffering. As the psychiatrist Thomas Fuchs argues, while the neurological turn in the treatment of "mental illness" appeared to have overcome mind–body dualism—insofar as the mind and the brain were to be unified as one system—what typically prevailed was a "neuroreductionist view" (Fuchs 2018, 253). Such an approach is characterised, according to Fuchs, firstly by a reduction of the mind to the brain, such that "mental disorders must be brain disorders" (2018, 253). Secondly, this reduction opens the way for a reification of "mental illnesses," whereby "a mental disorder must be more or less equivalent to either too high circuit activation, reduced metabolic activity, or some other dysfunction in certain areas of the brain" (2018, 253). Lastly, Fuchs states that these conceptual moves allow for the isolation, hence separation, of the individual sufferer from "his [sic] environment—even if it is conceded that the brain is epigenetically influenced by early life trauma or disturbed attachment relations" (2018, 253).

The recognition of the need to return the brain to the environment has manifested in calls to acknowledge the role of poverty, discrimination—at the intersections of race, sexuality, disability, and gender—ecological devastation, diet, and technological change in the development of "mental illness." Alongside Rasmus Birk and Nick Manning, the influential sociologist Nikolas Rose has argued for a neuroecosocial turn in psychiatry, one that would acknowledge the ways in which "mental illnesses" are formed through a group's interaction with their "environmental niche" (Rose et al. 2022, 123–124). According to Rose, Birk, and Manning, niches are understood, not only as the "mode of existence" of a group—including factors like "diet, temperature range, reproductive requirements"—but also as the spaces that particular groups co-produce for themselves, insofar as they attempt to build a coherent form of life (Rose et al. 2022, 124). Drawing on the work of human geographers, Rose, Birk, and Manning argue that such niches also reflect certain moods or what could be called "sensory environments," such that they are "atmospheric" and circumscribe those that inhabit their niche within "a mixture of affects and emotions, of feelings of calmness or excitement, of melancholy or joy, holiness or eroticism" (2022, 129). Furthermore, as such niches become unstable, the risk of the development of "mental illness" arguably increases. To this end, the attempt to resituate "mental illness"—and the brain as the supposed locus of such "illnesses"—within the group's encounter with, and co-production of, their environmental niche, is occurring alongside research into the impacts of global warming on "mental health" (Thoma et al. 2021; Cianconi et al. 2020; Wu et al. 2020). Recessions that require friends and families to uproot and search out new opportunities; bushfires and floods that destroy homes and places of cultural significance and render the air unbreathable and the land untraversable; viral pandemics that shut down the normal routines of life; and the more humdrum impact of traffic pollution and light pollution (Bogard 2014)—all of these phenomena are being reasserted as impacting the health of the mind.

Of course, one can still find discussions of "chemical imbalances" as the supposed cause of "mental illness" in popular and academic literature, and genes and neurotransmitters are far from marginal in the scientific and popular discourses of "mental health."[1] Nevertheless, a growing counter-discourse is placing renewed emphasis on the interrelations between the social, ecological, and economic, such that, if we are to continue discussing "mental illness" in terms of the brain, we face increased pressure to take seriously the network of relations that shape how the brain functions. Without for a moment diminishing the importance of scrutinising the methodological soundness, and broader epistemological value of such studies into the environmental determinants of "mental illness," the work cited here is useful, not because it reveals to us a hidden truth about "mental illness," but, instead, because it helps us to see a discursive shift that is occurring in the study of such existential suffering. Over the last few decades, the sense that many of the factors that precipitate "mental illnesses" are ambient—surrounding individuals in their everyday lives rather than originating from the internal spaces of the nervous system or brain—has become more common, and will perhaps become hegemonic. Despite these shifts in research foci, such discursive changes are of course not solely the result of research and debate within elite institutions and specialist academic fields. Instead, concomitant with the growing reconceptualisation of "mental illness" as what I am calling environmental illness are changes in the everyday utilisation of media to participate in forms of self-care and self-soothing. Not only have experts become more aware of the impact of the environment on the individual's mind and/or brain, that is, but non-experts have become more reliant on therapeutic and para-therapeutic media in the attempt to mitigate, if not control, the impact of the burden of relationality on the sufferer's thoughts and feelings. Indeed, not only is there a growing discourse that frames existential suffering as ecological—in the sense that "mental illnesses" and their causes are understood to be both increasingly ubiquitous and interconnected—there is also a range of "ambient media" that have been seized on by the public in the hope of reclaiming a sense of calm, security, and sanity.

Ambient Media

Before specifically discussing therapeutic ambient media, it will be helpful to first extend the precursory discussion of ambient media that was provided in the Introduction. Discussions of ambience have become prominent in a range of theoretical discourses, with the last 20 years seeing publications on the ambient character of rhetoric (Rickert 2013), the ambience of screens and televisual displays in the contemporary urban environment (McCarthy 2001; Papastergiadis 2016), and the broader shift towards ambient forms of culture and self (McCullough 2013; Roquet 2016). Shared by these texts is a concern for the ways in which various forms of media—and especially digital media—are becoming ambient; encircling, surrounding, or part of the background. To talk of ambient media, as James Miller states, "suggests a media history come full circle: if people once arrayed themselves around their media, the condition is now reversed, with media present in most aspects of social life" (Miller 2018, 383). A common example used to illustrate this point is the ubiquity of screens in the daily lives of hundreds of millions of people, with electronic messages presented on phones, tablets, on large displays in city squares, on the sides of buildings, and inside buses, trains, and cars. Whereas digital media might have once been immobile and situation-dependent—located within the fixed sites of the office, laboratory, living room, or home study—they now cover a wide range of surfaces; from walls to wrists; computers and their interfaces have become ubiquitous.

This might raise the question: Does the term ambient media simply refer to the digitisation of print and graphic media, since posters, fliers, road and street signs, and billboards have long been ambient, ubiquitous, and environmental? If we resist the urge to make arbitrary chronological distinctions about media—the kind of distinction that would maintain that an iPhone's screen is an interface, but a door or window isn't—what is so distinct about the mediated world of late modernity, such that the term ambient media is useful? If the ubiquity of media produces the experience of being surrounded—such that, as Alexander R. Galloway has put it, "the more intuitive a device becomes, the more it risks falling out of media altogether, becoming as naturalised as air or as common as dirt" (Galloway 2012, 25)—then surely newspapers, paperback novels, and print media street-directories are as ambient a form of media as anything produced in the twenty-first century. However, and despite the value of avoiding absolute or metaphysical distinctions between ambient media and other kinds of mass media or ubiquitous media, the former can aid us in understanding new modes of relationality, attention, and intimacy. While the forms of media described as ambient are perhaps better understood as a continuation and intensification of the prior cultures of "mass media," we can nevertheless see something distinct about the mediated condition labelled ambient.

For example, the relational qualities of ambient media are vastly more sophisticated than those associated with mass media, such as radio, television, or the conventional advertising billboard. As Nikos Papastergiadis, Amelia Barikin, and Scott McQuire argue, with regards to the "ambient screen" in urban settings:

> as the screen has become integrated into computational networks, it can also serve as a navigational tool, an archival depository, a platform for

communication with multiple partners, a tracking system that measures movements and augments the coordination of diverse elements in a complex system.

(Papastergiadis et al. 2016, 213)

Ambient media open up relational flows of data between individuals, between individuals and media, and between media themselves. Rather than communication being simply portable or situational—which has been the case for much of modernity—media can now relate data to us, to others who might wish to surveil or solicit, and to media that rely on their relationships with other devices to provide prompts and updates. As Deborah Lupton has detailed, self-tracking devices such as "wearables" allow individuals to record, share, and audit a staggering array of information about one's self and one's surroundings (Lupton 2016, 16–19). From health to finance, from one's emotional fluctuations to a daily step count, wearables allow for the production of increasingly detailed self-measurements. Furthermore, the relationships between such media are not only ambient in the sense that they permeate the ever-more aspects of our lives—becoming dispersed and pervasive; "as naturalised as air," as Galloway put it—but also insofar as they come to shape our field of relations in real time. An example of the latter was provocatively illustrated by the artist Simon Weckert, whose *Google Maps Hack* from 2020 saw Weckert pull a handcart of 99 smartphones through the streets of Berlin, causing Google Maps to report a traffic jam caused by 99 slow-moving vehicles, and which subsequently prompted drivers using Google Maps to select a different route to avoid the non-existent obstruction.[2]

In part, such relationality is afforded by ambient media's repositioning of the interface from the foreground to the individual's background or surrounds. As Malcolm McCullough writes, one early experiment in ambient media was the "Ambient Room" project at the MIT Media Lab in the 1990s (McCullough 2013, 26). Developed by the Tangible Media Group, Ambient Room experimented with models of communication that emphasised subtle shifts in environmental qualities, rather than the display of information in discrete and foregrounded screens or devices.[3] For example, rather than displaying information relating to the weather, stock prices, or the health of a loved one on a monitor that requires focused attention, the Ambient Room experimented with moving information to a ceiling screen or to dynamic airflow. As such, the inhabitant of the ambient media environment comes to an awareness of new information through a shift in the atmospheric qualities that are part of the background or are peripheral, purportedly freeing the inhabitant to focus their attention on other tasks. Information here surrounds the individual, rather than being limited to a focal point. As McCullough recounts, while these experiments may have been initially limited to small cubicle spaces—as one would encounter in an office setting—such an interest in moving information and relationships to digital media and to the background or surrounds, as opposed to the foreground and display, would itself extend further into larger terrains (McCullough 2013, 15). As McCullough writes:

> the expanding new field of *urban informatics* (also known as the *augmented city* or *urban computing*) seeks to collect, share, embed, and interpret urban infrastructural and environmental data. This agenda has become vital to the cultural imperatives of urban resilience, livability, and socialization. That makes interaction design ever more significant as a cultural endeavour, and more like architecture.
>
> (McCullough 2013, 16)

By increasingly moving into the background, ambient media allows for an increase in relationality, not only because the individual is purportedly free to shift their attention whilst also maintaining peripheral channels of communication, but also by opening exchanges of communication—albeit often unintended ones—with a range of different entities. Or, as Thomas Rickert puts it, and in a manner that accords with Hörl's conception of denaturalised ecologies, "we are entering an age of ambience, one in which boundaries between subject and object, human and nonhuman, and information and matter dissolve" (Rickert 2013, 1).

Arguably, it is through the dissolution of these boundaries that new styles of attention and intimacy emerge. As Pastergiadis et al. have argued, Walter Benjamin provides us with perhaps the first account of this change in attention (Pastergiadis et al. 2016, 217). As Carolin Duttlinger comments, whereas many of Benjamin's contemporaries, such as Siegfried Kracauer and Theodor W. Adorno "condemned mass culture as detrimental to the individual's reflective and critical faculties," Benjamin's work offers "an intriguingly versatile and complex" discussion of attention, such that attention and distraction enter into a complex dialectical relationship (Duttlinger 2007, 34).[4] Especially in "The Work of Art in the Age of Mechanical Reproduction," Benjamin argued that both ancient artforms such as architecture and modern artforms such as cinema promote distraction, not simply as the absence of attention or the inability to concentrate, but rather as an alternative mode of attention (Benjamin 2007, 239–240). Or as Pastergiadis et al. put it in their reading of Benjamin:

> in presenting us with an early vision of what we call ambient awareness, Benjamin suggests how the process of discernment requires an ability to stretch consciousness, derive information from multiple reference points, including new visual technologies such as photography and cinema, and thereby develop a sensibility that can merge with this field.
>
> (2016, 217)

In Pastergiadis et al.'s reading of Benjamin, architectural spaces and cinematic screenings do not promote the kind of focused attention that painting or sculpture might command (2016, 216). The scale of the architectural interior, and the speed at which a film combines images, hinders fixed attention and encourages an "ambient awareness" in which the viewer perceives:

> by relating elements that are peripheral to each other and organizing them into a new form. The forms that emerge are in themselves also fleeting and contingent. They do not emerge from a fixed point or return to a central hierarchy.
> (Pastergiadis et al. 2016, 218)

While Benjamin was likely aware of the tourist who might make a point of stopping to view a piece of architecture as if it were a painting or sculpture—focusing on a particularly elaborate piece of brickwork, for example—and while we are today aware that an individual can pause, rewind, and fast-forward a piece of video—so that one could conceivably focus on an individual frame of a film as if it were a painting—these are exceptions to the way such media are conventionally apprehended. Moreover, and perhaps more importantly, in "The Work of Art in the Age of Mechanical Reproduction," Benjamin employs a distinction between the contemplative attention of the individual and the distracted attention of the masses. As he puts it:

> a man who concentrates before a work of art is absorbed by it [*Der vor dem Kunstwerk sich Sammelnde versenkt sich darein*]. He enters into this work of art the way legend tells of the Chinese painter when he viewed his finished painting. In contrast, the distracted mass absorbs the work of art [*Dagen versenkt die zerstreute Masse ihrerseits das Kunstwerk in sich*]. This is most obvious with regard to buildings. Architecture has always represented the prototype of a work of art the reception of which is consummated by a collectability in a state of distraction.
> (Benjamin 2007, 239)[5]

In this illustration, we find the individual concentrating before a work of art such that their attention is consumed—they are "taken in" or absorbed by the work of art, so to speak. Contrastingly, the masses, through their distracted mode of shifting attention, work to "take in" the "artwork"—for example, in the way one might struggle to look around the 360 degrees of the architectural space, struggling to "take it all in" before the tour guide moves on. While any piece of mass media can be approached in terms of the individual act of concentrated focus—where one arrests their spectatorship, and concentrates on discrete features—such acts of attention arguably detract from the mass character of the media. Walking through the lobby of a building, or sitting amidst a rapt crowd in a theatre, the distracted mode of attention is massified, and, thereby, it is also one that surrounds or is ambient. As Schmidt puts it, the ambient experience involves a simultaneous "spreading out" of attention and of the things to be attended to, insofar as within the mediated environment there is "a close link between the spreading out of a given structure and the spreading out of the experience of that structure" (Schmidt 2013, 180).

Today, smartphones and wearables allow for such ambient awareness even when the individual is separated from the mass or crowd. Watching a movie alone in one's living room, the presence of social media via a smartphone allows one to connect to the thoughts and feelings of the crowd. Indeed, it is common for fans to "livetweet" their reactions to television shows, engaging in collective forms of response and interpretation on social media, such that one engages in a kind of mass distraction—or what the linguist Michele Zappavigna has called "ambient affiliation" (2011)—albeit through forms of mediation markedly different from those discussed by Benjamin in the 1930s. Of course, the capacity to engage in a distributed collective reading of a text creates barriers to the kinds of close reading one would associate with focused attention. Nevertheless, such networked forms of attention allow for new forms of intimacy and togetherness, such that "people who are constantly ping-ponging text messages to each other claim to feel 'ambient intimacy'" (Pastergiadis et al. 2016, 218). Checking in with family and friends via text messages, or liking and sharing posts made on social media, wearables and smartphones have allowed millions the opportunity, not only to stay connected, but also to share intimate details without necessarily engaging in concentrated and delimited acts of dialogue or closeness. Arguably, such new opportunities for intimacy change the way we understand the world emotionally. Just as ambient attention functioned through the logic of distraction, ambient intimacy involves the apprehending of moods and emotions through peripheral details. Or as Pastergiadis et al. put it,

> without being physically side by side, people become adept at picking up a mood. They may not know the source, recognize the total configuration, or even pick the precise turning point in a specific sequence of events, but by stitching together numerous microdetails they form an overall impression.
> (2016, 218)

The notion that one's mood, can be recorded, conveyed, and measured—and from various peripheral data points that are spread out across a range of interactions—without the need for conventional forms of attention or intimacy underpins the recent explosion of ambient therapeutic media. Championed for being cheaper, more accessible, and more effective, a range of ambient media have been seized upon as a way of increasing well-being and "mental health."

Ambient Therapies

Within medical research, the precursor to what I refer to as ambient therapeutic media is arguably the ecological momentary intervention, or EMI.

The coining of the term EMI is attributed to public health researcher Kevin Patrick and his co-authors in a 2005 paper (Patrick et al. 2005). While their paper focused on media that might assist in communicating information relevant to the prevention and treatment of cancer, the notion of EMIs has had a broader influence in medical research. The prediction made in 2005 was that individuals would increasingly have access to portable computers that would allow for the quick dissemination of health information (Patrick et al. 2005). Beyond this, Patrick and his team wondered whether such technology could receive information from the user and their environment, such that it could genuinely respond to the user's surrounds rather than providing readymade facts (Patrick et al. 2005, 7). Of course, with the development of smartphones, smartwatches, and other wearable technologies, Patrick and his team's speculations have become more enticing for another generation of medical researchers.

As argued by Myin-Germeys et al., researchers are increasingly looking for ways to use EMIs in order to extend a patient's therapy "beyond the clinical setting into real life" (2016, 258). Or, as Andreas Balaskas et al. put it, today "the argument is that these systems provide the capability to deliver psychological intervention strategies at opportune moments, in real-world settings, and in an accessible and scalable fashion" (Balaskas et al. 2021, 2). While this transposition of therapy into "real life" has mostly focused on what are understood to be somatic health issues, such as "diabetes, asthma, weight loss, or smoking," the cheapness of EMIs in comparison to conventional talk therapy, the way EMIs can assist in prompting users to maintain psychopharmacology regimens, and the promise of more individually tailored treatments have created optimism for the advancement of EMIs into the terrain of "mental health" (258–59). But what do EMIs for "mental health" look like in practice? Myin-Germeys et al. provide the example of the FOCUS smartphone application, which is:

> specifically developed to provide automated real-time and real-world illness management support to individuals with schizophrenia. FOCUS consists of five modules targeting medication adherence, coping with symptoms, mood regulation, sleep problems, and improving social interaction. For each module, evidence-based techniques such as cognitive restructuring, behavioural tailoring, social skills training, anger management, sleep hygiene, and behavioural activation are implemented. For each patient, three of these five modules are selected: medication adherence and two other "high priority" areas.
>
> (Myin-Germeys et al. 2016, 259)

Applications like FOCUS illustrate the becoming-ambient of "mental health" therapeutics in at least two ways. Firstly, such media offer the promise of therapy on demand, as wearables and smartphones allow for assistance with mood tracking, "mental health" training or coaching, and contact with fellow users or chatbot "therapists." As Emma Bedor Hiland has shown in her study of emerging "mental health" technologies, *Therapy Tech: The Digital Transformation of Mental Healthcare*, applications and platforms such as 7 Cups, Woebot, Wysa, and Joy—to name only a few available—are marketed in terms of their capacity to provide perennial support, their portability, and their negligible cost (2021). As the promotional copy for Woebot claims on the Apple App Store, "there's no need to struggle alone, Woebot is there for you 24/7 whether you're looking for guidance, growth, or just a chat, you've got an expert in your pocket whenever you need it."[6] Accordingly, the therapeutic relationship is no longer limited to the private space of the therapist's or psychiatrist's office. Instead, "mental healthcare" is becoming increasingly ambient, something that can be called upon in a wider array of settings and at almost any time. Besieged by a panic attack on a bus, or waking to feel the psychomotor retardation characteristic of major depression, the user of an application like Woebot is able to access a basic therapeutic response within minutes, if not seconds. As such, therapy can meld into the background as a service to be called on when needed, rather than as a focused activity that requires a dedicated time and space.

Beyond the increased ubiquity of such mediated therapy, EMIs and ambient media reveal the becoming-ambient of "mental health" in a second way, insofar as they further reinforce the understanding of "mental illness" as ecological. As Myin-Germeys et al. argue, "moving therapy out of the office into real life is more than just changing the delivery modus," and must also involve an increased awareness of the "dynamics between the person and his/her environment that may be at the core of psychiatric symptoms" (Myin-Germeys et al. 2016, 262). As I have suggested, the acknowledgement that "mental illness" is influenced by a range of environmental factors—including diet, noise and light pollution, social interactions, or weather, only to name a few elements—provides further impetus for self-tracking and psychosurveillance. Not only do today's "mental health" technologies offer one the possibility of responding to an experience of depression, anxiety, and potentially even psychosis "on the move" by way of human and non-human forms of ambient intimacy, but they also offer systematic ways of recording and analysing the environmental factors that precipitate episodes of poor "mental health." As such, the origins of "mental illness" become intelligible as relations that occur through one's surrounds, and in the present, insofar as one's present living environment, microbiome, working environment, and social milieu are related to "mental illness" as much as one's past or, as with Freudian-inspired psychotherapies, one's childhood may have been understood as primordial space or time of an emerging "mental illness." Or, put differently, the earlier emphasis on relationality that one finds in much psychoanalytic literature is expanded into an ambient or ecological sense of relationality—not just the relations of intersubjectivity, but also the relations of the human and non-human.

As we will go on to discuss in subsequent chapters, this rise of an increasingly mediated and ecological understanding of "mental illness"—in other words, an understanding that is ambient—is not limited to applications explicitly marketed as curative or ameliorative and thereby explicitly part of "mental healthcare." Furthermore, the use of gamification in a range of "mental health" applications assists in reframing everyday, or potentially overlooked, activities as forms of therapy or treatment. For instance, the use of common gamification elements such as "levels or progress feedback, points or scoring, rewards or prizes, narrative or theme, personalization, and customization" can assist in motivating individuals to take a walk, talk to a friend, take their medication, meditate, or participate in any number of therapeutic and paratherapeutic activities (Cheng et al. 2019, 8). As such, one's journey towards better "mental health" and well-being becomes pursuable at all times and in all spaces, which is to say ambient, or atmospheric.

While it is tempting to view this becoming-ambient of therapy as primarily produced by changes in media, it is arguable that these aforementioned shifts are inseparable from far earlier changes in our understanding of therapy and attention. Just as ambient media can be seen as a continuation and intensification of earlier forms of mass media, ambient therapeutics maintain a certain degree of resonance with the psychotherapies of the earlier twentieth century. Indeed, one could argue that the two interconnected Freudian ideas of "evenly suspended attention" and "free association" bear something of a resemblance to Pastergiadis et al.'s and Schmidt's readings of Benjamin's notion of distracted attention. For Freud, it was vital that the analysand's tendency for unconscious and conscious censorship be overcome by encouraging a specific form of attention, one that privileged the relay of free-floating ideas and associations. As Freud put it, the analyst should aim to produce "a heightening of the patient's attention so far as his psychical perceptions are concerned and a switching-off of the critical faculty with which he is otherwise in the habit of inspecting the thoughts that occur to him" (Freud 2006, 113). In the context of dream interpretation, for instance, Freud encouraged the analysand to avoid making "the whole dream the object of attention" and instead to attend to "only individual bits of its content" (Freud 2006, 116). Comparable to Pastergiadis et al.'s aforementioned discussion of ambient intimacy as involving the "stitching together [of] numerous microdetails" in order to form an "overall impression," the injunction to "free associate" seems to involve a similar search for a logic of attention other than that of focused and delimited concentration. Furthermore, Freud advised analysts to adopt a kind of "evenly suspended attention" in their practice. As Freud writes:

> for as soon as anyone deliberately concentrates his attention to a certain degree, he begins to select from the material before him; one point will be fixed in his mind with particular clearness and some other will be

correspondingly disregarded, and in making this selection he will be following his expectations or inclinations.

(Freud 2001, 112)

Accordingly, Freud's emphasis on a loosening of concentrated attention—such that the analysand's unconscious processes might become visible, and so that the analyst does not overeagerly impose an interpretation on such processes—could suggest that the digital shift towards ambient attention and intimacy does not represent an absolute break with the past. There are of course considerable differences between the kind of attention, intimacy, and even subjectivity produced through ambient media and Freudian psychoanalytic traditions—differences that we will explore further in the book's conclusion. Nevertheless, it would be hasty to argue that the becoming-ambient of attention, intimacy, and therapy can be explained through an appeal to technologically deterministic narratives. Instead, it is perhaps more sensible to acknowledge ambience as a mediatic possibility that has persisted alongside other logics of attention and intimacy, albeit one that has become increasingly dominant over the last 50 years. This dominance has been met with a great deal of scepticism in the critical literature. For a range of thinkers, what we have been calling the becoming-ambient of therapy should be understood as the expansion of neoliberal conceptions of selfhood and sociality to the spheres of "mental health."

Ambient Media as Neoliberal Self-Governance

From a certain perspective, Deleuze's and Guattari's figure of the schizophrenic—who is "out for a walk" and enjoying "a breath of fresh air" and "a relationship with the outside world"—has been realised in the user of a "mental health" application like FOCUS. No longer restricted to the analyst's couch—or the psychiatric hospital—such an application offers the possibility of freedom, mobility, and something like a therapeutic phase change, with solid boundaries transformed into vaporous atmospheres. From another perspective, such an application could also be interpreted as symptomatic of what Deleuze would later refer to as "societies of control." Writing in the 1990s, Deleuze raised concerns around the atmospheric, dispersed, and modular forms of power that characterised life in the late twentieth century. Indeed, Deleuze concludes his short text *Postscript on the Societies of Control* by discussing a "control mechanism," a device that would give "the position of any element within an open environment at any given instant" (1992, 7). Reframed as a "control mechanism," the FOCUS app could be seen to allow the sufferer of schizophrenia to enjoy a greater sense of freedom and autonomy, while greater aspects of their life are infused with coercion and control. Indeed, while in the aforementioned *Therapy Tech*, Emma Bedor Hiland maintains it is possible that the increasing availability and adoption of "mental health" monitoring and surveillance, facilitated by an array of technologies including social media algorithms and wearable devices capable of digital phenotyping, might normalize and destigmatize mental distress and illness" it is far more likely that such media will be used as a form of control, one that will see "discrimination based upon presumptions about our "mental health" and aptitudes for violence based on the medicalization of collected information" (2021, 146). For Bedor Hiland, while we cannot know how dominant "mental health" applications will be in the future, they already "function as apparatuses of social control" and are inseparable from the promotion of individualism and self-responsibility as "neoliberal values" (2021, 146).

In his narration of the emergence of neoliberalism, Grégoire Chamayou states that the 1970s revealed an interlinked crisis of governability, one that involved both those who were tasked with governing, and those to be governed (2021, 3). Against the relative prosperity and stability of the post-WWII "Keynesian consensus" or the *"trente glorieuse,"* the economic and political crises of the 1970s, coupled with the protest movements against racism, colonisation, patriarchy, capitalism, and war—and against the incarceration and mistreatment of those with "mental illness"—revealed a political and economic class that was losing its capacity to govern, and various populations unwilling to be governed in the old ways. As Chamayou writes, "the problem was not only that people were growing rebellious, nor just that the apparatuses of government were congested, but that these failures and revolts overdetermined each other, weighing down on the system to the point of bringing it close to collapse" (2021, 3). Drawing on Foucault, Chamayou argues that some new form of governance had to emerge in order to stabilise this double crisis. A new way of negotiating economic instability and political radicalism, on one hand, and maintaining the liberal emphasis on freedom and progress, on the other, was needed. Not only would this need result in the emergence of new and novel ways of conceiving of property, institutional and corporate management, politics, and markets, but it would also see the emergence of new forms of subjectivity—new patterns of conduct, and new norms around what is existentially and conceptually possible and desirable at the level of individual and collective life.

The increased emphasis on individual happiness (Binkley 2014; Davies 2015), self-responsibility and resilience (Rose and Lentzos 2017), and education and health as forms of human capital (Brown 2015; Russell 2018), are all well-documented aspects of this new form of neoliberal subjectivity—or what Bedor Hiland summarises as "neoliberal values." However, these new forms of subjectivity have not been without their tensions and antinomies. As Alain Ehrenberg has argued in his sociological history of the explosion of depressive disorders in the twentieth century, the 1960s were replete with demands to overthrow the disciplinary regimes of modernity, such that "unprecedented moral freedom united with improved economic conditions, and the opening of lifestyle choices, always upwardly mobile, became a tangible reality during that decade" (2016, 228). For Ehrenberg, this period was epitomised by the belief that "everything was possible" (2016, 228) and the demand for the recognition and acceptance of difference was married with various attacks on government bureaucracy and elitist institutions. During this time, notes Ehrenberg, "mental illness" was viewed as a form of difference to be emancipated from the paternalistic and cruel state (2016, 228), and, as Andrew Scull's historical research can help us to see, a combination of psychopharmaceutical innovation, a desire to curtail excessive state expenditure on asylums and mental hospitals, and the radical critiques of the exclusion of the "mentally ill" from community and civil society saw a dramatic decline of the psychiatric hospital as a disciplinary apparatus (Scull 2016, 369–378). However, such liberations from discipline have been marked by deep ambivalences. As Ehrenberg notes, the prevalent belief in the 1960s that everything is possible has increasingly given way to the twenty-first-century sense that "nothing is possible." As Ehrenberg writes:

> people feel as though they have collapsed into the present. The shutting down of the economy and the dropping out of a segment of the population reinforces this feeling. The demands on our cognition are many. The theme of respect-the-limits runs up against the collective aspirations of those who want no limits placed on their freedom of choice.
>
> (2016, 228)

It would seem then that the simultaneous breakdown of institutional spaces of discipline, and the proliferation of new techniques of self-governance, helped to intensify the tensions between freedom and recognition and between self-efficacy and reciprocity. As the sociologist Andreas Reckwitz has argued, whether we understand the citizen as a rational consumer maximising their investments and satisfactions, or, in a more progressive vein, as an individual in search of recognition of their particular identity and concomitant rights, the end result is a social field in which "there no longer seems to be any room for society as a space of reciprocity—that is, a space for mutual social benefits, with laws and obligations that seek a balance between one's own individual interests and those of others" (Reckwitz 2021, 168). Close to Ehrenberg's analysis, Reckwitz views the late twentieth-century and early twenty-first-century culture of self-actualisation—inspired greatly, on Reckwitz's account, by positive psychology—as ironically functioning to produce powerful negative feelings. As he writes:

> in the bright light of public attention, late-modern culture dances around the golden calf of "positive emotions" and yet, at the same time, furtively gives rise (not coincidentally, but systematically) to intense negative

emotions. The latter are based on the disappointment that is induced by perceived discrepancies between expectations and reality. The experiences of disappointment generated by late-modern culture are intricately connected to strong negative feelings: to various shades of anxiety, sadness, or rage.

(Reckwitz 2021, 121)

Accordingly, various critical accounts of the concomitant rise of neoliberal subjectivity and ambient therapeutic media—both of which place a great emphasis on atomised individualism against the mass conformity and hierarchy of the disciplinary apparatus—suggest a kind of positive feedback loop in which projects of self-governance that aim to improve the "mental health" of the individual arguably create a greater propensity for negative emotions and experiences of unfreedom.

In this way, while Deleuze's "Postscript on the Societies of Control" can be read as a corrective to Foucault's work on disciplinary power—and the emphasis, in such work, on the "enclosures" of such a regime of power: the factory, school, hospital, prison, etc.—Foucault's *College de France* lectures still have a great deal to teach us about a still-emerging form of power that is ecological and ambient. As Erich Hörl argues, Foucault, in his 1978–79 lectures, outlined a transition from "individualizing (internal) subjugation, which produces the subject of the disciplinary society, to (external) Environmentalization" (2018, 159). While Foucault "did not and could not explore in detail the operating systems of environmental technologies, which at the time were only just entering the scene" Hörl nevertheless argues that Foucault's reference to B.F. Skinner in the 1978–79 lectures provides us with greater access to his thought on "environmentality" (2018, 159). As Hörl observes, while Skinner is often understood as a behaviourist, he could also be classified as an "environmental psychologist" insofar as Skinner's *Walden II* engaged directly with the impact of an organism's environment on its behaviour (2018, 160). Following Foucault, Hörl argues that psychology would greatly contribute to the emergence of "environmentality," insofar as it would increasingly reconceptualise subjectivisation as the process of an environment's influence on the individual organism. Or, put differently, psychology would help to transform the control of behaviour by reemphasising the necessity of controlling the organism's environment, rather than guiding conduct through conditioning at the individual level.

With regards to the genealogy of environmental subjectification, Hörl points out that Foucault's 1978–79 lectures coincide with the publication of Harvard psychologist James Gibson's *The Ecological Approach to Visual Perception*, a text that emphasised the centrality of the environment to human perception (2018, 160). As Gibson argued in the introduction of his text, laboratory studies of visual perception had traditionally emphasised focused attention, insofar as the "headrest, the bite-board, the exposure device, the tachistoscope, the darkroom with its points of light ... made it possible to study vision *experimentally*" (2015, xv). But insofar as "the headrest of the laboratory prevents the observer from turning his head and looking around," commented Gibson, such laboratory approaches modelled human perception on the camera, with visual perception understood to be "compounded of units like a snapshot" (2015, xiv). Against the study of vision that requires "the subject to fixate a point," and which produces what Gibson dubbed "*snapshot vision*," he hoped to study perception married with movement and awareness of the surrounds, "the kind of vision we need in life" and that Gibson referred to as "*ambient vision*" and "*ambulatory vision*," respectively (2015, xiv). However, more than simply aligning his experimental research with the broader shifts from focused attention to ambient distraction—as discussed in this chapter—Hörl views Gibson's research as being paradigmatic of a shift in viewing organism and environment as entwined, and environments as modifiable. As he writes, "in Gibson, there is no separation between natural and artificial environments; he thinks only in terms of transforming, not to say modulating, environments" (2018, 160).

One of Foucault's key insights in his 1978–79 lectures was that this new form of power as environmental modulation would open up greater tolerance for marginality and difference. As he writes, the society that was then emerging in the late 1970s was one in which "minority individuals and practices are tolerated" since "the exclusion of those who cannot be normalised" is no longer unavoidable (Foucault 2010, 259). With the increased acceptance that "mental illnesses" are in fact "environmental illnesses"—that is, problems arising at the level of relationality—it becomes ever more possible to accept "mental illness" as a form of difference—albeit a form of difference that is continually and ambiently nudged and guided by way of the mediated environment. As such, a range of critics have raised concerns around the use of what we have been calling ambient media, insofar as the latter often functions as a form of subjugation that is difficult to detect—"as naturalised as air or as common as dirt," to again quote Galloway (2012, 25). Ambient media, and the conceptualisation and treatment of "mental illnesses" as "environmental illnesses," have provoked some scholars to critique the mediation of "mental healthcare" as an extension of neoliberal governance and subjectification.

Indeed, for Hörl, once the process of subjectification is understood environmentally—and once coupled with "the ubiquity of digital media technology" that we have referred to as ambient—the becoming-environmental of the self creates the conditions for new forms of governance—forms of governmentality that threaten to become forms of what he calls environmentalitarianism (2018, 155). Likening the latter to Shoshana Zuboff's notion of "surveillance capitalism," environmentalitarianism is discussed in terms of the commodification and accumulation of human experience, with reality itself falling prey to the logics of utility and optimisation (Hörl 2018, 161)—an issue we will return to in Chapter 4 when we discuss QAnon and online sociality. As Zuboff argues, firms like Google have based their business model on the extraction of a "behavioural surplus" that emerges through the incidental data generated by its users. No longer content to utilise such data to improve their services, Zuboff accuses Google of increasingly manipulating such data in order to predict and even steer the user's conduct (Zuboff 2019, 78). As such, while the intervention by technology companies in "mental healthcare" is a unique application of ambient media, it is arguably part of a much vaster system of control—one in which individual thoughts, feelings, and behaviours can be steered through the manipulation of what is experienceable through a digitally mediated environment. As more and more behavioural data are captured through ambient therapeutic media, it is possible that logics of extraction and accumulation will require individual conduct to be steered—more or less imperceptibly—towards those forms of life that expand surplus value.

Such pronouncements present a bleak picture of ambient media and ecological logics of subjectivity. The move away from the asylum and the arguably elitist understandings of treatment that emerge through mainstream psychiatric and psychoanalytic knowledge is potentially giving way to a dispersed and yet quasi-incontestable form of ambient power over life. On Hörl's reading, what we have been calling ambient media can be understood as expanding a logic of environmentalitarianism, such that our ever-expanding relationships to other humans and non-humans become a means for extraction and exploitation. The modes of attention and intimacy privileged by ambient media and discussed in this chapter—aiding in the dispersal and multiplication of attention and intimacy across a diverse range of phenomena—arguably accelerates such exploitation. Moreover, "mental illness" potentially features in these new environments of control as a unique site of governance—one that often necessitates radical behavioural modification on behalf of the sufferer, whilst also providing unique data on the complex relationships between human and non-human entities that precipitate existential suffering. Nevertheless, there are many scholars who view ambient media and ecological notions of the self as potentially emancipatory, and as offering counterhegemonic modes of conduct that cannot be neatly circumscribed within neoliberal systems of governance. As we will go on to discuss in Chapter 3, a range of contemporary media and social theorists view the emerging eco-logics of subjectivity as opening up the individual to modes of relationality that are underpinned by an ethics of care and empathy.

However, before we can assess such accounts it will be vital to develop a more theoretically robust theory of environmental illness. If environmental illness implies a shift away from biologically and psychologically reductive accounts of "mental illness" towards more expansive notions of the complex human and non-human relations that constitute "mental illness," and if ambient media can provide new and emancipatory relations between the human and non-human, then we will need to understand what such a logic of relationality entails. Accordingly, in the next chapter we will turn to German sociologist Hartmut Rosa's major work *Resonance: A Sociology of Our Relationship to the World* in order to expand our discussion of environmental illness in terms of Rosa's account of alienated and non-alienated logics of relationality.

Notes

1 Consider, for example, the fallout from Moncrieff et al.'s systematic umbrella review of the evidence for the serotonin hypothesis of depression (2022). While many took this publication to be the final nail in the coffin of the popular notion that depression is caused by a chemical imbalance, a range of commentators have responded by reaffirming the efficacy of antidepressant drugs, even if their therapeutic function remains mysterious. Regarding the latter, see Davey (2022).
2 For more information on this artwork, see: www.simonweckert.com/googlemap-shacks.html.
3 For a helpful video overview of the Ambient Room experiment, see: https://tangible.media.mit.edu/project/ambientroom/.
4 Duttlinger notes that Benjamin attempted to embrace distraction in the production of his *oeuvre*, such that he embraced "more provisional, fragmentary modes of reflection" in his discussions of culture, politics, and history (Duttlinger 2007, 51). In the highly thought-provoking conclusion to her essay, Duttlinger argues that Benjamin's embrace of distraction as a mode of reception complicated the reception of his own work, not only by his peers, but also by contemporary readers (Duttlinger 2007, 51). For some, Benjamin's methodological embrace of fragmentation must be resisted through a subjection of individual texts "to a kind of contemplative meditation" in the hope of producing "a coherent theoretical edifice" (Duttlinger 2007, 51). For others, Benjamin's approach is embraced as proof of his status as "the precursor of postmodern arbitrariness, fragmentation, and distraction" (Duttlinger 2007, 51). The problem, as Duttlinger sees it, is that "both approaches … fall short of the challenge whose fruitful yet deeply precarious implications are exemplified by Benjamin's own writings: to maintain a form of attentiveness whose openness towards the marginal, the overlooked, and the forgotten collapse neither into solipsistic absorption nor into endless dispersal" (Duttlinger 2007, 51). I linger on this point because, as we will see in the ensuing discussion, the account of Benjamin provided by Pastergiadis et al. perhaps aligns itself too neatly with the "postmodern Benjamin," such that it is worthwhile acknowledging that compelling and yet contrastingly systematic readings of Benjamin exist. As we will see, the problem of this perhaps false choice between solipsistic absorption and endless dispersal resonates with the broader aims of this book, and will be returned to in subsequent chapters.
5 For the German text, see Benjamin (1963).
6 https://apps.apple.com/us/app/woebot-your-self-care-expert/id1305375832. Accessed April 30, 2022.

References

Balaskas, Andreas, et al. 2021. "Ecological Momentary Interventions for Mental Health: A Scoping Review". *PLoS One* 16.3: 1–23.

Benjamin, Walter. 1963. *Das Kunstwerk im Zeitalter seiner technischen Reproduzierbarkeit*. Frankfurt: Suhrkamp.
Benjamin, Walter. 2007. *Illuminations: Essays and Reflections*. Ed. Hannah Arendt. Trans. Harry Zohn. Berlin: Shocken Books.
Bogard, Paul. 2014. *The End of Night*. London: Fourth Estate.
Binkley, Sam. 2014. *Happiness as Enterprise: An Essay on Neoliberal Life*. Albany: State University of New York Press.
Brown, Wendy. 2015. *Undoing the Demos: Neoliberalism's Stealth Revolution*. New York: Zone Books.
Chamayou, Grégoire. 2021. *The Ungovernable Society: A Genealogy of Authoritarian Liberalism*. Oxford: Polity Press.
Cheng, Vanessa Wan Sze, et al. 2019. "Gamification in Apps and Technologies for Improving Mental Health and Well-Being: Systematic Review". *JMIR Mental Health* 26.6: 1–15.
Cianconi, Paolo, et al. 2020. "The Impact of Climate Change on Mental Health: A Systematic Descriptive Review". *Frontiers in Psychiatry* 11: 74. doi: 10.3389/fpsyt.2020.00074
Davey, Christopher. 2022. "The Chemical Imbalance Theory of Depression Is Dead – But That Doesn't Mean Antidepressants Don't Work". *The Guardian*, 3 August. https://www.theguardian.com/commentisfree/2022/aug/03/the-chemical-imbalance-theory-of-depression-is-dead-but-that-doesnt-mean-antidepressants-dont-work
Davies, Will. 2015. *The Happiness Industry: How the Government and Big-Business Sold Us Wellbeing*. London: Verso.
Deleuze, Gilles. 1992. "Postscript on the Societies of Control". Trans. Martin Joughin. *October* 59: 3–7.
Deleuze, Gilles, and Guattari, Félix. 2009. *Anti-Oedipus: Capitalism and Schizophrenia*. Trans. Robert Hurley and Helen R. Lane. London: Penguin.
Duttlinger, Carolin. 2007. "Between Contemplation and Distraction: Configurations of Attention in Walter Benjamin". *German Studies Review* 30.1: 33–54.
Ehrenberg, Alain. 2016. *The Weariness of the Self: Diagnosing the History of Depression in the Contemporary Age*. Trans. Enrico Caouette, Jacob Homel, David Homel, and Don Winkler. Montreal: McGill-Queen's University Press.
Foucault, Michel. 2010. *The Birth of Biopolitics: Lectures at the College de France 1978–1979*. Trans. Graham Birchell. London: Palgrave Macmillan.
Freud, Sigmund. 2001. *The Standard Edition of the Complete Works of Sigmund Freud Volume XII: Case History of Schreber, Papers on Technique and Other Works*. Trans. James Strachey. London: Vintage.
Freud, Sigmund. 2006. *Interpreting Dreams*. Trans. J.A. Underwood. London: Penguin.
Fuchs, Thomas. 2018. *Ecology of the Brain: The Phenomenology and Biology of the Embodied Mind*. Oxford: Oxford University Press.
Galloway, Alexander. 2012. *The Interface Effect*. Oxford: Polity Press.
Gibson, James J. 2015. *The Ecological Approach to Visual Perception*. London: Psychology Press.
Insel, Thomas. 2022. *Healing: Our Path from Mental Illness to Mental Health*. New York: Penguin.
Hörl, Erich, 2018. "The Environmentalitarian Situation: Reflections on the Becoming-Environmental of Thinking, Power, and Capital". *Cultural Politics* 14.2: 153–173.

Hiland, Emma Bedor. 2021. *Therapy Tech: The Digital Transformation of Mental Healthcare*. Minnesota: University of Minnesota Press.

Lupton, Deborah. 2016. *The Quantified Self: A Sociology of Self-Tracking*. Oxford: Polity Press.

McCarthy, Anna. 2001. *Ambient Television: Visual Culture and Public Space*. Durham: Duke University Press.

McCullough, Malcolm. 2013. *Ambient Commons: Attention in the Age of Embodied Information*. Cambridge, MA: MIT Press.

Miller, James. 2018. "Media and Mobility: Two Fields, One Subject". *Journal of Transport History* 39.3: 381–397. doi: https://doi.org/10.1177%2F0022526618793396

Moncrieff, Joanna, Cooper, Ruth E., Stockmann, Tom, et al. 2022. "The Serotonin Theory of Depression: A Systematic Umbrella Review of the Evidence". *Molecular Psychiatry* https://doi.org/10.1038/s41380-022-01661-0

Myin-Germeys, Inez, et al. 2016. "Ecological Momentary Interventions in Psychiatry". *Current Opinion In Psychiatry* 29.4: 258–263.

Papastergiadis, Nikos. 2016. *Ambient Screens and Transnational Public Spaces*. Hong Kong: Hong Kong University Press.

Papastergiadis, Nikos, et al. 2016. "Conclusion: Ambient Screens". In *Ambient Screens and Transnational Public Spaces*. Ed. Nikos Papastergiadis. Hong Kong: Hong Kong University Press. 211–238.

Patrick, Kevin, et al. 2005. "An Ecological Framework for Cancer Communication: Implications for Research". *Journal of Medical Internet Research* 7.3: 1–8.

Reckwitz, Andreas. 2021. *The End of Illusions: Politics, Economy, and Culture in Late Modernity*. Trans. Valentine A. Pakis. Oxford: Polity Press.

Rickert, Thomas. 2013. *Ambient Rhetoric: The Attunement of Rhetorical Being*. Pittsburgh: University of Pittsburgh Press.

Roquet, Paul. 2016. *Ambient Media: Japanese Atmospheres of the Self*. Minneapolis: University of Minnesota Press.

Rose, Nikolas, et al. 2022. "Towards Neuroecosociality: Mental Health in Adversity". *Theory, Culture & Society* 39.3: 121–144. doi: https://doi.org/10.1177/0263276420981614

Rose, Nikolas, and Lentzos, Fillipa. 2017. "Making Us Resilient: Responsible Citizens for Uncertain Times". *Competing Responsibilities: Ethics and Politics of Contemporary Life*. Eds. Susanna Trnka and Catherine Trundle. Durham: Duke University Press. 27–48.

Russell, Francis. 2018. "Wages for Self-Care". *Cultural Studies Review* 24.2: 26–38. https://doi.org/10.5130/csr.v24i1.5582

Schmidt, Ulrich. 2013. "Ambience and Ubiquity". In *Throughout: Art and Culture Emerging with Ubiquitous Computing*. Ed. Ulrich Ekman. Cambridge, MA: MIT Press. 175–188.

Scull, Andrew. 2016. *Madness in Civilisation: A Cultural History of Insanity, from the Bible to Freud, from the Madhouse to Modern Medicine*. London: Thames & Hudson.

Thoma, Myriam V., et al. 2021. "Clinical Ecopsychology: The Mental Health Impacts and Underlying Pathways of the Climate and Environmental Crisis". *Frontiers in Psychiatry* 12: 675936. doi: 10.3389/fpsyt.2021.675936.

Wu, Judy, et al. 2020. "Climate Anxiety in Young People: A Call to Action". *The Lancelet: Planetary Health* 4.10. doi: https://doi.org/10.1016/S2542-5196(20)30223-0

Zappavigna, Michelle. 2011. "Ambient Affiliation: A Linguistic Perspective on Twitter". *New Media & Society* 13.5: 788–806.

Zuboff, Shoshanna. 2019. *The Age of Surveillance Capitalism: The Fight for a Human Future at the New Frontier of Power*. London: Profile Books.

2 Mute Instruments and Resonant Relations

As Eva Giraud summarises in her critical study of contemporary environmental and posthuman thought, *What Comes After Entanglement? Activism, Anthropocentrism, and an Ethics of Exclusion*, the last three decades have seen the emergence of "a burgeoning body of work" that emphasises "the ways that human existence has *always* been knotted together with the lives of other entities" (2019, 5). Perhaps exemplified by Bruno Latour's actor-network theory (2007), Donna Haraway's "tentacular thinking" (2016), and Karen Barad's agential realism (2007), this heterogenous body of work is nevertheless held together by a commitment to "decentering the human as the locus for ethics and politics through recognizing—and often celebrating—relationality" (Giraud 2019, 6). Or, with reference to Haraway, we could state that such approaches are aligned insofar as they pose the question, "what happens when human exceptionalism and bounded individualism, those old saws of Western philosophy and political economics, become unthinkable in the best sciences, whether natural or social?" (Haraway 2016, 30).

Given, then, that relationality has become such a central concern within the works of figures so influential in fields such as animal studies and the environmental humanities, it might seem odd to turn to the work of Harmut Rosa in order to expand our aforementioned discussions of environmental illness. Unlike Latour, Haraway, or Barad, Rosa's work does not show an obvious affinity with questions of environment or ecology, nor is his work especially influential in discussions of posthumanism or in critical accounts of "mental illness." While Rosa, Christoph Henning, and Arthur Bueno have drawn attention to similarities between contemporary critical theory and relational philosophies, such as new materialism, of importance for this project is the emphasis on normative accounts of social existence—something arguably lacking in new materialism—that we can find in the work of a figure like Rosa (Rosa, Henning, and Bueno 2021, 3). As Rosa, Henning, and Bueno have stated, while new materialism has helpfully indicated some of the potential shortcomings of the tradition of critical theory—such as its potentially "uncritical adoption of dualisms that tend to subordinate matter to spirit, the biological to the social or affectivity to rationality"—the trio nevertheless

DOI: 10.4324/9781003215202-3

maintain that new materialism's "attempt at avoiding dualisms entails an abandonment of distinctions that might nevertheless prove crucial for social critique as well as for its own project" (2021, 7). In particular, Rosa, Henning, and Bueno raise concerns around new materialism's allergy to normative assessments of ideology, insofar as they view figures like Latour as mocking ideology critique as part of the "'cult' of 'anti-fetishism'" (2021, 8).

Neither Latour's work nor new materialism can be seen as synonymous with the broader theoretical interest in relationality and entanglement in the contemporary humanities. Likewise, Rosa's work cannot be made synonymous with contemporary critical theory *tout court*. Nevertheless, Rosa's work distinguishes itself amongst many influential contemporary theories of relationality insofar as it maintains a clear commitment to a normative account of human happiness, the good life, and a possible overcoming—if not completely, then at least situationally—of alienation. Indeed, at first glance Rosa's interest in the concept of alienation—a major preoccupation in *Resonance*—may strike readers of contemporary theory as oddly antiquated and humanistic, insofar as alienation is often viewed as a relic of a surpassed twentieth-century Marxist humanism or, worse, conservatism. Despite this, through his concept of resonance, which I will spend the majority of this chapter unpacking, Rosa attempts to reestablish a social theory of the good life that is non-metaphysical and pluralistic. Rather than pointing to an unalienated content of a particular form of life, Rosa's project in *Resonance* is to describe a form of relationality that can emerge in heterogenous contexts, but that is nevertheless recognisable as necessary for human happiness and well-being. Indeed, in developing this account of unalienated relationality, or resonance, Rosa provides a novel, if not underdiscussed, theory of "mental illness" as relational. Accordingly, in this chapter, I will emphasise those moments in Rosa's *Resonance* that explicitly take up the social origins of "mental illness" in order to develop a critical account of environmental illness, one that will allow me, in the third chapter, to explore the question of ambient media's purported emancipatory and counterhegemonic potential.

Resonant Relationality

For Rosa, one of the chief failings of contemporary sociology is its inability, or unwillingness, to entertain a positive conception of the good life (2019, 23). On Rosa's account, "modern mainstream sociology" is hindered by maintaining a scepticism regarding philosophy's normative claims about reality—viewed by sociology as overly theoretical and lacking in empirical evidence—and psychology's account of experience—viewed by sociologists as overly subjective and unreliable (2019, 23). Accordingly, on the question of the state of contemporary societies, Rosa laments sociology's inability to do much more than "observing and measuring inequalities in resources" and using this as a proxy for gauging levels of individual happiness (2019, 23).

While Rosa is quick to emphasise the dangers of culturally arbitrary notions of the good life, he nevertheless argues that sociology can provide a broad account of the kinds of societies and existences that we should be collectively moving towards. For Rosa, what structures the good life is a high level of what he refers to as resonance. As Rosa puts it, resonance can be defined as:

> a specifically cognitive, affective, and bodily relationship to the world in which subjects are touched and occasionally even "shaken" down to the neural level by certain segments of world, but at the same time are also themselves "responsively," actively, and influentially related to the world and experience themselves as effective in it—this is the nature of the responsive relation or "vibrating wire" between subject and world.
>
> (Rosa 2019, 163)

It is worth emphasising that resonance denotes a "relationship" and not a particular experience, mood, or worldview (Rosa 2020b, 398). As such, a sunny disposition does not necessarily indicate a relation of resonance, and a lugubrious outlook does not necessarily preclude resonance—as, again, the form rather than the content of relationality is key for Rosa (Rosa 2019, 174). Accordingly, Rosa's analysis engages both the individual's relationship to the world, and the constraints placed on the world by particular social structures or institutional forms. Rather than emphasise individual psychology or the superiority or inferiority of particular outlooks, Rosa places an emphasis on various institutional forms—and whether such forms promote or discourage resonance (Rosa 2019, 397–400). As Rosa notes, while virtually all institutions promote various forms of sensitivity to otherness and mindful relationships to the self and world, under the conditions of capitalism this promotion is typically underpinned by a logic of accumulation and intensification, such that even sensitivity and mindfulness become instrumentalised in the pursuit of profit or rankings (Rosa 2019, 400). For this reason, while an individual might obtain a psychological experience of openness, the institutional context allows for the world to be accessed primarily in instrumental terms—thereby rendering it mute and closed off in terms of possibilities for reciprocity or resonance. Put differently, the affirmation of resonance does not limit itself to demanding a change in the individual's ways of thinking and acting, but instead questions the capacity for institutional arrangements to open up resonant modes of comportment.

As such, a resonant relationship is one in which subject and world are both open to one another and can be mutually or reciprocally transformed, in which subject and world maintain sufficient identity to be able to speak "*with their own voice,*" such that neither is trapped within an echo chamber, nor is subsumed entirely into the other (2019, 174). Vital, for Rosa, is the development of a social theory that can critically explore the institutional arrangements and cultural formations that impede resonance as a mode of subject–world relationality. Through such a social theory, Rosa's account suggests, we can move beyond the limitations of a mere accounting of differences in assets or habits of consumption, which he views as a dominant but extremely limited method for assessing the success or failures of various societies. Against an emphasis on how much individuals earn, the extent of their educational attainment, or the length of their lives, a theory of resonance has the potential to anchor a critical account of society in terms of what, for Rosa, makes life truly meaningful and worth living.

To this end, Rosa begins his book with a series of literary vignettes designed to illustrate the difference between a mute and resonant relationship to the world. In one of these vignettes, Rosa introduces us to Adrian and Dorian. Adrian graduates high school to become a prosecutor. He is an atheist and prefers a scientific outlook on life devoid of romanticism or mysticism, and outside of his demanding work he enjoys holidaying in large cities and speculating on the stock market (2019, 10). Dorian, by contrast, studied art, history, and German literature at university, and eventually became a teacher. He enjoys taking long hikes in mountainous regions, and is a practicing Catholic (2019, 10). While Rosa acknowledges the stereotypes smuggled into these personae, he nevertheless uses Adrian to illustrate the mute relationship to the world, and Dorian to illustrate the resonant relationship to the world. In the courtroom, Rosa tells us, Adrian can only act "strategically, manipulatively, and instrumentally," since any attempt to act with "empathy or compassion, understanding or accommodation" will potentially weaken one's argument and chance of legal victory (2019, 11). Again, by contrast, Dorian works in a school and finds in the classroom a space of "genuine sympathy and concern, and the ability to both touch and be touched" (2019, 11). The fundamental difference between these two spaces, for Rosa, is that the classroom allows for resonance, for us to appropriate our context and to be appropriated by it, whereas the courtroom is a mute space, with each party acting instrumentally and seeking only to appropriate their surrounds for personal gain, rather than as a means of being caught up in something larger.

Rosa acknowledges that his examples are somewhat arbitrary, and that it would be possible to retell his vignettes such that the classroom is a space of instrumental strategising, and the courtroom a space for mutual recognition, appropriation, empathy, and resonance. Nevertheless, Rosa intends such illustrations to simply show that resonance is prior to and more significant than other normative concepts that might be used to articulate a conception of the good life, such as meaning or happiness. A key limitation of these concepts, on Rosa's account, is their relatively autonomous status within the modern context. Since at least the Enlightenment, argues Rosa, the question of whether or not a life is a happy one or a meaningful one has been disconnected from any notion of a natural *telos* or goal (2019, 18). Against a hegemonic notion of what human life aims towards in terms of successful completion or maturation, liberal societies increasingly affirmed the notion that "*everyone must know for themselves what they want to make of themselves and their lives*" (2019, 18). As such, the question of happiness and meaningfulness becomes increasingly disconnected from the norms of religion or tradition, becoming individual and autonomous in the process. However, Rosa points out that such individual autonomy occurs within two key institutional and structural arrangements, those of acceleration and competition (2019, 21). On this account, while the procession of liberal modernity allows individuals greater autonomy over what counts as a meaningful or happy life, such meaning and happiness is underpinned by logics of acceleration and competition that see greater levels of activity and investment required in order to maintain even prior levels of happiness or meaning.

Of fundamental concern for Rosa is the fact that the autonomy or freedom to determine one's own happiness or meaning does not necessarily preclude an alienated relationship to the world. The only way to overcome alienation is, for Rosa, resonance. Or, as Rosa writes, "if acceleration is the problem"—although perhaps Rosa should have written if acceleration and competition are the problem—"then resonance may well be the solution" (2019, 1). Accordingly, in the next section, I turn to discuss Rosa's theory of alienation in order to better understand why he emphasises resonance as a truly counter-hegemonic and emancipatory mode of relationality.

Resonance and Alienation

As Rosa acknowledges, for much of the twentieth century, alienation was viewed as a pseudo-philosophical concept. Beyond observing that, at least by the mid-twentieth century, alienation had become a vague and overused term. Rosa notes that alienation has lacked a clear antonym that would act as its conceptual ground (2019, 175). Put differently, if the logics of acceleration and competition associated with modernity—or, more specifically, capitalist modernity—have caused immense human suffering, it is not at all clear that such suffering has alienated humanity from some essence or natural state. Especially for those influenced by Louis Althusser's anti-humanist Marxism—which argues that Marx's work from 1845 "broke radically with every theory that based history and politics on an essence of man" (Althusser 2005, 227)—alienation became something of an ideological concept that invoked metaphysical assumptions about what human life was in an idealised past or what it should be in an idealised future. As Emil Øversveen puts it, for most of the late twentieth and early twenty-first centuries, notions of human nature open to alienation are "associated with political conservatism as they are often invoked to either justify the existing social order or to argue a return to more earlier and traditional ways of human life" (2022, 443).

The justification of injustice and violence by way of an appeal to the need to reinscribe an alienated human nature of course holds a strong affinity with critiques of psychiatric knowledge and practice. Indeed, *alienist* is an antiquated term for psychiatrist, and, drawing on Foucault, one could argue that alienation—whether taken in the idiom of critical theory or the idiom of psychiatry, that is to say *aliénation mentale*—is a discourse historically and institutionally produced, rather than a state of separation from one's nature. As Foucault argues in his *History of Madness*, alienation as madness or insanity did not preexist the institutional forms of exclusion, categorisation, and knowledge production that would later become the asylums of Europe, but, instead, emerged through such institutional spaces of exclusion (2009 [1961], 80). The challenge presented by figures like Foucault with respect to both alienation as madness or insanity and alienation as a general exclusion from human nature is one of tarrying with a plurality of alienations that themselves belong to singular histories. Put differently, after Foucault—and others, including Althusser, of course—if we aim to utilise alienation as part of critical discourse, the latter term can no longer be viewed as a general and transhistorical state of privation from human nature. Instead, alienation would have to be seen as a mode of comportment amongst others, and, importantly, a mode of comportment divorced from any notion of an abandoned or unrealised essence or nature.

Despite these considerable theoretical problems, recent publications in contemporary critical theory evince an interest in a post-metaphysical rehabilitation of the concept of alienation. Perhaps the most influential work of this kind is Rahel Jaeggi's *Alienation*, which has clearly influenced Rosa's development of the concept of resonance. In *Alienation,* Jaeggi attempts to articulate a theory of the titular concept that neither is burdened by the legacies of humanist metaphysics nor aids a conservative project of Western chauvinism or paternalism. As Jaeggi puts it:

> alienation critique today cannot, but also need not be grounded in strongly essentialist or metaphysical presuppositions; moreover, it cannot but also need not rely on perfectionist or paternalistic arguments. The rich social and ethical dimension of alienation critique can be made accessible without the strongly objectivistic interpretive scheme that is frequently associated with it. And it is possible to avail ourselves of the critical import of the concept of alienation without relying on the certainty of a final harmony or reconciliation, on the idea of a fully self-transparent individual, or on the illusion of having oneself and the world completely at one's disposal or command.
>
> (2016, 32)

The problems posed by paternalism, essentialism, and holism have fuelled an aversion to alienation critique in contemporary theory, and, as such, Jaeggi acknowledges the difficulty of avoiding conservatism and cultural chauvinism when attempting to articulate a conception of non-alienated human life. Indeed, the more that we attempt to understand contemporary society, and the myriad modes of conduct that it facilitates, the more difficult it becomes to locate the natural, the self-identical, and the authentic. "The more human nature is given a specific content such that it becomes relevant to (culturally specific) forms of life" writes Jaeggi, "the more controversial and contestable the claims [regarding alienation] become" (2016, 30). Accordingly, Jaeggi's task is to develop an account of alienation that does not begin from the existence of a natural or essential content, but instead takes a "procedural or formal orientation" to the question of alienation (2016, 40). While it is not possible here to provide a comprehensive overview of Jaeggi's formal orientation, I will nevertheless summarise some key attributes.

Firstly, Jaeggi argues that alienation is partly determined by a relationship between the self and the world that is not characterised by acts of *appropriation*. By appropriation Jaeggi refers to the individual's capacity to practically engage with the world, to identify with one's actions—to see them as one's own—and in such a way that those actions are mutually transformative (2016, 37–38). By mutually transformative, Jaeggi means the capacity for the individual to leave their stamp on the world, but without one's actions resulting in an instrumental use of what is external to oneself—that is to say, without reducing others or other things to the status of passive objects. As Jaeggi states, appropriation involves both "penetration and assimilation" insofar as "appropriation always means a transformation of both poles of the relation" (2016, 38). Put simply, Jaeggi's account of appropriation describes a relation between the self and the world where the self can actively produce a place for themselves, and in which the world can transform the self that it accommodates.

Jaeggi's formal orientation has influenced Rosa at least insofar as it has provided an alternative that seems to avoid the essentialism, paternalism, and cultural chauvinism of earlier notions of the non-alienated life. Whereas past philosophers and theorists have turned to human nature, meaning, authenticity, and autonomy as potential categories to help identify the unalienated life, Rosa draws on Jaeggi to develop a relational account of alienation as a "relation of relationlessness" (Rosa 2019, 178). As Rosa puts it:

> alienation can be said to be overcome whenever and wherever subjects, in the course of a given interaction, are touched or affected by an Other or by others, and, moreover, are themselves capable of touching or affecting others; wherever one's relationship to the world and thus also to oneself appears to be at least potentially fluid or liquefiable.
>
> (Rosa 2019, 179)

If alienation is understood as a relation of relationlessness, then alienation is absent in those relationships defined by reciprocity and mutual transformation—that is, *resonance*. While Rosa's project is not primarily one of providing a new theory of "mental illness," his rehabilitation of alienation as various disruptions to the experience of resonance provides us with a means of better articulating an ecological theory of "mental illness," that is to say, environmental illness. Returning to Hörl's observations about ecological reason mentioned in Chapter 1, if ecology is becoming increasingly denatured—such that it is understood in terms of our mediated relationships rather than any connection to a natural environment—an environmental or ecological approach to "mental illness" would privilege the study of different kinds of relationality. As such, Rosa's understanding of depression, for example, avoids both biologism and a narrow and arbitrary account of unalienated life. Arguably, Rosa's emphasis on relationality allows him to overcome biologically or sociologically reductive explanations of "mental illness." As discussed in the previous chapter, biologistic accounts of "mental illness" run the risk of, if not ontologically, then at least practically, reducing human suffering to the physical functioning of the brain and thereby typically rely on psychopharmaceutical therapies. While critiques of biologistic accounts of "mental illness" have become more conventional—especially given the publication of popular texts such as Mark Fisher's *Capitalist Realism* (2009) or the *New York Times* bestseller *Deaths of Despair and the Future of Capitalism* by Anne Case and Angus Deaton (2020), both of which articulate the recent explosion of "mental illnesses" in terms of social dysfunction caused by late capitalism—less common are critiques of sociological reductionism. Indeed, while it is becoming more common to find critiques of the ever-increasing pace of contemporary life and the superficiality of contemporary consumer culture, such accounts pose the risk of popularising a caricature of the contemporary subject of alienation.

One of the advantages of Rosa's account is his attempt to provide a relational theory of "mental illnesses," whilst maintaining a plurality of experiences of alienation within contemporary society. In *Resonance*, drawing on the work of German psychoanalyst Fritz Riemann, Rosa articulates four alienated modes of relating to the world: those characterised by too much or too little attachment, and those characterised by too much or too little order or structure (2019, 113). According to Rosa, an individual can struggle to resonate with the world around them because they find their relationships to be all-consuming and without the space for the individual to express agency or autonomy (excess of attachments) but, depending on their circumstances, they could just as easily find the world to be too open to the point of seeming barren and empty insofar as their relationships are overly flexible and modular, if not capricious (lack of attachments) (2019, 113). Regarding order or structure, the individual can find the world to be oppressively structured and administered (excess of structure) or they could find the world to be on the brink of chaos (lack of structure) (2019, 113). While this quadripartite account is admittedly schematic, it is nevertheless useful for privileging neither anomie nor cultural chauvinism, bureaucracy nor anarchy, as the source of contemporary alienation. Instead, Rosa argues that all four of these axes—with possible meeting points in between—represent different breakdowns of resonance. Furthermore, Rosa argues that such forms of alienation can be used to understand the common forms of "mental illness" experienced in contemporary neoliberal societies.

We can better understand Rosa's relational theory of "mental illness" if we unpack two examples from *Resonance*, depression and anorexia nervosa (AN). Regarding depression, Rosa argues that this commonly experienced "mental illness" can be understood in terms of the breakdown of genuine attachments to others, the world, and even oneself (2019, 113). In the depressive position, one's relationships are relationless insofar as they are characterised by a lack of authentic or spontaneous attachment to others, resulting in feelings of loneliness, isolation, and futility. As Rosa writes:

> the extent to which nearly all symptoms of depression may be interpreted as symptoms of a comprehensive loss of resonance is frankly remarkable. Individuals suffering from burnout or depression experience the world as flat, mute, cold, and hollow, no longer capable of affecting them. At the same time, they also have lost the ability to emotionally move toward the world, toward people and things, and even toward the future, so that time itself appears frozen, with no "relationship" existing between past, present, and future. And because they have also lost any resonant relationship to their own body and feelings, they even perceive themselves as lifeless, dead, empty, and cold. Insofar as one's resonant wire thereby becomes rigid and inflexible at both ends, subject and world lose their colour and sound in equal measure. This, metaphorically speaking, is the core of a relationless relation, which can be observed in and measured by, among other things, the extent to which individuals suffering from severe depression lose their capacity for bodily resonance.
> (Rosa 2019, 179–180)

Here, Rosa is aligned with phenomenological research into the experience of depression, such as the work of Matthew Ratcliffe. As Ratcliffe has observed, while we often describe depressed people as being cut off or isolated, it is just as common for the depressed to encounter others as hostile and threatening (2015, 141). As Rosa has argued, it is not the case that one is simply unable to enter into relationship with others, but, instead, that one's relationships are characterised by intense negative affects. As Ratcliffe writes, citing an interview subject suffering from depression, "people change from being people who I love and am connected with to being hosts of a parasite—me. I can't see why anyone would like me, want me, love me" (2015, 141). What is lost or missing, then, is not the relation itself but the capacity for the individual to experience such a relation as entailing reciprocity and an intertwined mutability. As Ratcliffe writes, depression is not so much the failure to relate to others, but, instead, "an all-pervasive *way* of relating to others" (2015, 141).

Alongside this alienated form of relating to others, Rosa draws on AN as an example of an alienated relationship to oneself and one's body. As Rosa argues, while the instrumentalisation of the body is "neither necessarily pathological nor specifically modern" what is perhaps unique to modernity is the reframing of the body as both a resource or asset to be invested in, and as an entity that we are somewhat removed from (2019, 104–105). To illustrate this point, Rosa provides the distinction between the embodied act of manual labour, and the somewhat disembodied act of manipulating a computer (2019, 104). On Rosa's view, whereas manual labour involves the body directly in the intentional act—of digging or planting, for example—when manipulating a computer, the body recedes into the background as a mere prerequisite for action (2019, 104). Although Rosa does not unpack this point, he seems to view modernity—and especially late modernity—as involving an excess of opportunities to relegate the body to a mere background prerequisite for action, and, accordingly, as a potential site of frustration and inhibition that conflicts with our desire for control and agency. Ironically, however, Rosa's discussion of the late modern body as a prerequisite or background for action also entails an increased foregrounding of the body once it has failed or frustrated us. Put differently, Rosa's account suggests that a disembodied detachment from our corporeal selves can also encourage an objectification of and fixation on the body in the form of a granular scrutiny of our appearance, weight, and stamina. In this way, for Rosa the view of the body as something to be optimised and controlled—rather than something we are as embodied beings—precipitates alienated relationships to oneself, such as those labelled as AN (2019, 105).

While Rosa's discussion of AN is brief and somewhat abstract, we can find support for his account in recent work by the philosopher Lucy Osler. According to Osler, the common conception of the AN sufferer involves the assumption that the individual experiences their body in a distorted way, such that their (potentially emaciated) body appears as too large. As Osler observes, conventional ways of understanding and treating AN, especially via cognitive behavioural therapy, frame AN as a product of "faulty or disruptive thoughts, beliefs and judgments," especially relating to the size of the individual's body (Osler 2021, 54). While Osler is careful to not discount the existence of this kind of AN, she nevertheless complicates it as a dominant framework by arguing that the attempts to cognitively redress AN run the risk of missing its underlying logic (Osler 2021, 54). Rather than resulting solely from a misunderstanding or faulty experience of one's body—an image of the sufferer of AN that, as Osler points out, is made famous by numerous cinematic depictions, in which a typically female individual stares into a mirror to be met by an overweight if not obese image of themselves—AN can also be understood as a complex and overdetermined intolerance of the uncontrollability of one's corporeal self. However, for Osler, a fixation on thinness perhaps distracts us from the logics of self-control that seem to underpin many of the comportments associated with AN. As Osler argues, several first-person and academic accounts of AN explore the disorder as first involving a period of feeling empowered—in control of one's body and therefore one's self—and yet this initial period is typically followed by a sense of losing control over one's attempts at self-control, before finally entering an obsessional phase (Osler 2021, 46).

In her article, Osler draws heavily from Marya Hornbacher's book *Wasted*, a memoir about struggling with anorexia and bulimia. In this memoir, Osler notes the repeated use of sonic language, with the body described, not as too large, but as loud, noisy, and out of control. As Osler writes, "Hornbacher describes how she experienced her body as something loud, domineering, threatening; something that she was unable to trust or block out" (2021, 46). "The individual with AN, as an act of self-preservation, attempts to control and silence the noisy demanding body in search"—so Osler observes—"of a radical embodiment as a body-as-subject, freed from the demands of the physical body" (2021, 46). Rather than allowing the body to resonate, to speak to us in its own voice and yet in a voice we can hear and respond to in a relationship of mutual transformation, Osler highlights how AN involves an experience of the body's "voice" as noise—as something to be controlled or silenced. Interestingly, and as sound studies scholar Robin James has pointed out, noise takes on a new meaning in twentieth-century thought and culture, such that whether one is discussing macroeconomics or avant-garde composition, noise is no longer "an impediment to be eliminated (e.g., harmonized away by some sort of invisible hand or perfect authentic cadence) but something that can be accounted for and rendered productive" (2019, 25). From stochastic modelling in finance, to the harsh noise of a music producer like Merzbow, a capacity to engage with excesses of information can become both esteemed and lucrative in late modernity. Similarly, the AN sufferer does not exclusively respond to the noise of the body through strategies of silencing and repression, but, instead, often draws on such noise to engage complex regimes of self-scrutiny and research. As Osler writes elsewhere alongside Joel Krueger, AN can involve:

> obsessively weighing and scrutinizing one's body in front of the mirror or taking selfies to find flaws; maintaining a diary of desired body-focused improvements; using technologies for hyperdiligent calorie counting; developing complex, excessively intricate eating rituals (supported by various artifacts and technologies) intended to slow down the eating process and minimize consumption; regularly inhabiting online spaces (pro-anorexic websites, blogs, social media, or chat groups; image-blogging platforms like Instagram and Tumblr) for tips, strategies, inspiration, or emotional support.
>
> (2020, 259–260)

Following this argument, it would appear that attempts to control and manipulate the noisy body—to be freed from unwanted or unintended demands, faults, or weaknesses—create a positive feedback loop of further intolerance, which, tragically, can result in a complete inability to hear the body, and therefore the self, on its own terms. Similarly, Rosa argues that AN should be understood as an alienated form of world appropriation. Rather than being the result of a disordered relationship to food *per se*, AN is instead, on Rosa's account, an alienated relationship to the world, insofar as a sense of insecurity in the face of the world's uncontrollability manifests in drives for self-control that, ironically and tragically, are themselves further sources of instability and insecurity (Rosa 2019, 61).[1] Following Rosa and Osler, then, we can see the embrace of self-control as potentially precipitating deeply unsettling and painful relationships to oneself, others, and the world. Insofar as one's self and one's surrounds become an object to be instrumentally manipulated, the individual in question perversely exposes themselves to powerful feelings of alienation and discomfort.

Accordingly, while Rosa does not discount the biological dimension of alienation—quite the opposite, as embodiment is a central theme running throughout *Resonance*—his account of "mental illnesses" as alienation nevertheless emphasises the failures of relationality that many individuals encounter in their lives. In both the example of depression and AN, the "mental illness" in question is characterised by a particular alienated relationship between self and world rather than a specific breakdown of an internal biological mechanism. Moreover, while this explanation is sociological it does not reify a particular mode of sociality as all-pervasive, such that Rosa's account can explain, at least taken on its own terms, why certain individuals experience "mental illness" and not others, despite sharing an existence that is circumscribed within the logics of neoliberal governance. Accordingly, and as I will discuss further in the next section, despite being a marginal theme in *Resonance*, we can read Rosa's emphasis on particular breakdowns of relationality as providing an account of "mental illness" as environmental illness.

From Alienation to Environmental Illness

Up until this point in my discussion of Rosa's work, one could counter that *Resonance's* contribution to our conceptual understanding of "mental illness" is marginal, especially when compared to the emphasis on intersubjectivity found within various forms of psychoanalysis and social psychiatry. While it is true that the analysis of relationships has long been a focus of the psy-sciences, Rosa's approach seeks to emphasise the importance of resonance with non-human entities and forces as much as the conventional psychiatric study of human intersubjectivity. As has been discussed at the beginning of this chapter, Rosa feels that there is an affinity between the work of new materialists like Karen Barad, Donna Haraway, Jane Bennet, and Paul Rekret and contemporary approaches to critical theory such as his own. Following Rosa, Henning, and Bueno, we can argue that Rosa's concept of resonance aims at something similar to the new materialist project of attempting to produce "feelings of kinship, closeness and 'response-ability' not only toward fellow human beings and animals but also toward landscapes, microbes, and even the universe as a whole" (2021, 7). We can perhaps see this most clearly in Rosa's discussion of nature as a "potential source of resonance" and the absence of such relationships to nature as a potential source of alienation or "mental illness" (2019, 272).

Rosa links the everyday desire for connection to the non-human—whether through adorning one's office space with pot plants, walking and hiking around local vegetation, living with pets or feeding local animals like birds, seeking out "natural remedies," or learning about the natural world—to a desire for a relationship with something "inaccessible, wilful, and yet also responsive to our actions" (2019, 272). The absence of such resonance, Rosa argues, leaves individuals and communities with a powerful sense of anxiety in the face of a world that feels increasingly unresponsive. The importance of resonance, and the fear that industrial capitalism might permanently destroy the potential for maintaining a resonant relationship with nature, should be, on Rosa's account, more central to discussions of climate change and ecological devastation. As Rosa writes:

> modernity's fundamental anxiety with respect to the environment" should not be understood as the disappearance of key resources, but the fear that "nature might fall mute as a *sphere of resonance*, an independent counterpart capable of responding to us and thus giving us some orientation.
> (2019, 274)

Indeed, for Rosa, the increased desperation that many feel in encountering nature as responsive expresses itself symptomatically through the "growing concerns about the ongoing destruction of the environment and fears of nature taking 'revenge' in the form of tsunamis and tornadoes, avalanches and earthquakes, heatwaves and droughts" (2019, 428). Rosa is not referring to those who directly encounter such devastation—thereby having no need for an ulterior reason to fear nature—but instead to the vast numbers of people who live more or less shielded from the direct impact of climate change. Here, Rosa's work provides us with an interesting alternative explanation for the popularity the natural disaster film genre has held with the public over the last few decades. While, as Claire Colebrook has argued, climate disaster films present us with the fantasy of being able to "anticipate and master an event that concerns our (in this case, very real and possible) non-existence" (2014, 187), following Rosa, we can suggest that such media also present us with a world in which nature maintains its voice—a world in which nature can respond, even if violently, thereby countering anxieties of a world that has become mute.

However, given that we have argued for a reading of Rosa's interconnected theories of resonance and alienation as non-metaphysical and non-essentialist, how are we to understand the reference to nature as a sphere of resonance? What *is* nature if it is not taken to be something homeostatic, self-identical, and pure? While Rosa does not offer us a particularly robust or detailed theoretical account of nature—beyond referring to a fairly expansive notion of the non-human realm—I would argue that nature as a sphere of resonance is much closer to Isabelle Stengers's notion of Gaia than it is to commonsense understandings of the natural world, and scientific understandings of nature as a physical system. For Stengers, global warming has revealed to us a new being, "Gaia," which, as the "living planet" itself, is utterly without the possibility of stability or homeostasis (Stengers 2015, 47; 2018, 136). Gaia, in the context of Stengers's texts *In Catastrophic Times* and *Another Science Is Possible: A Manifesto for Slow Science*, is a name intended to highlight and give some theoretical force to a being without intentionality, a being that is in a sense radically indifferent to human life, and yet still requires us to respond (2015, 43–46). Gaia is accordingly not the earth as a calculable physical system, nor is it our "mother" or home. Instead, on Stengers's account, the earth or "Gaia" is a dynamic being we endure alongside, replete with powers to affect and change, although in such a way that is radically irreducible to human plans, stories, or hopes (2015, 46–47). One could argue that Stengers's notion of Gaia—in contrast to conventional uses of the term nature—refers to a being of dynamism and excess, and one that will be felt by way of its continual disruptions and insistences. As such, the earth must now be understood, in the wake of huge ecological disruption, to insist and intrude into our lives as a "major unknown" (2015, 47).

Rosa would perhaps agree. His account of resonant relationships with nature are not reducible to fantasies of a harmonious primordial connection between mother and child. As Rosa writes, "resonance thus can never exist where everything is [in] 'pure harmony,' nor does it arise simply from the absence of alienation. It is rather a *flash of hope for adaptive transformation and response in a silent world*" (2019, 187). For Rosa, a resonant relationship with nature constitutes a dynamic and open relationship in which the human and non-human can speak to each other with their own voices, and enter into mutually transformative dialogue. A preestablished harmony would not leave room for the distinctiveness of these voices, and, accordingly, Rosa's account resists a nostalgic longing for a premodern view of nature as humanity's mother or guardian. Indeed, the specific content of this dialogue, or the specific tenor of these voices, is something Rosa attempts to leave in suspension so as to avoid reinforcing hegemonic cultural ideals—especially Eurocentric ones. Accordingly, since a resonant relationship with nature could take the form of an encounter with an enlivening breeze through the window of a cramped inner city apartment window, just as much as a walk through a forest or the delightful surprise of a cat bounding onto one's bed, Rosa's account is useful, not because it reminds us of the benefits of swimming at the beach or gardening for our "mental health," but because it helps to reframe the very problem of "mental illness" as relational—and with a concept of relationality that includes the non-human world. For Rosa, what has been traditionally viewed within late modernity as a "psychological crisis," or a "mental illness epidemic"—to use a term popular in news media—is inseparable from an environmental crisis (2019, 377). Although this is not Rosa's explicit intention, we can read this environmental crisis as being irreducible to the narrow understanding of ecological collapse, but as involving a crisis at the level of relationality itself—a crisis in the form of a mass alienation that results from the struggle to form open, transformative, and reciprocal relationships within and between the spheres of self, society, and the non-human. As Rosa writes, the crisis of modernity—while usefully partitioned into the study of failing liberal democratic states, failing ecosystems, and failing psychological identities—are fundamentally underpinned by a "widespread crisis of resonance" (2019, 377).

However, while Rosa consistently emphasises the formal character of relationality as his key concern—that is, the critique of relations in terms of their resonant and alienated form, and not in terms of their specific content—there is nevertheless one area where he maintains a surprisingly normative view of the relata in question. Consistently throughout *Resonance*, Rosa casts doubt over the role of what we have called ambient media in modern society. Although careful to avoid a totalising critique of such media, Rosa nevertheless identifies ambient media as producing what could be called pseudo-resonance—spaces that function more like echo chambers than "true" spheres of resonance.

Ambient Media and Resonance

Rosa's critique of the relationality offered by ambient media is best understood in the context of the account of ambient media as neoliberal self-governance discussed in Chapter 1. As the influential sound studies scholar Michael Bull has argued, the development of media such as personal stereos, mobile phones, and physical media and device-connective stereos in cars has greatly expanded the capacity for individuals to curate their own sonic and affective environments (Bull 2004, 2013). Arguably, the smartphone has combined these earlier media into a central device for affect curation, with headphones, speakers, wearables such as smartwatches, and virtual assistants connecting via the smartphone. While this centralisation of media within the one device—albeit a centralisation that has ironically facilitated greater dispersion and mobility, or ambience—could make Bull's analysis appear outdated, I would argue that it has only become even more relevant for understanding the formation of the neoliberal subject. As Bull argues, "the attempted exclusion of all forms of intrusion constitutes a successful strategy for urban and personal management, a re-inscribing of personal space through forms of 'sound' communication. In so doing, users re-claim representational spaces precisely by privatizing them" (Bull 2004, 288).

While Bull does not explicitly discuss neoliberalism, much contemporary media theory has sought to critically examine the becoming-ambient of media in the hope of showing the inextricable connection between neoliberal governance and what are now dominant notions of affective curation and emotional self-regulation. As Bull writes:

> the sound of the personal stereo is direct, with headphones placed directly in the ears of the user, thereby overlaying the random sounds of the environment passed through with privatized sounds. Personal stereo users construct their own privatized and intimate space of reception.
>
> (2004, 283)

He goes on to cite the testimony of one of his interview subjects, Catherine, in support of this point: "it fills the space whilst you're walking. It also changes the atmosphere. If you listen to music you really like and you're feeling depressed it can change the atmosphere around you" (2004, 283). Accordingly, while more specialised ambient media for "mental illness" can be found in the form of applications like Woebot, we can see a folk-therapeutic use of more ubiquitous media such as smartphones and noise cancelling headphones. Such an experience will be shared by many, as music, podcasts, or even a phone conversation can soothe an anxious or wearied mind during a bus or car ride home after a stressful day of work. While the availability and almost universal adoption of such technologies can render them banal, it is worthwhile reflecting on the relative novelty of this kind of affective curation. Indeed, media platforms such as Spotify provide the listener with such an expansive archive of sonic media that it has become common to organise playlists around moods as opposed to genres, eras, or personal collections. As Jeff Gage writes for the *Washington Post* (2022) a mood-based muzak playlist like "Peaceful Piano" holds its own against hugely popular genre mixes like "Rock Classics"—with "Peaceful Piano" holding 6.8 million subscribers, and "Rock Classics" 11.2 million subscribers on Spotify as of the time of writing. Spotify provides listeners with playlists like "Chill Vibes" or "Sad Moody Mix," and Spotify users share playlists such as "Oh you don't even smile/Music to immerse yourself"—a mix of downtempo electronic music—and "Brazilian Doomer Music"—a playlist of melancholic Bossa Nova tracks. While it is of course true that the use of music to curate affects, and even the production of music for instilling specific moods is of course not new—one only has to think of the production of Bach's Goldberg variations, which were allegedly commissioned to treat insomnia—the portability, customisability, and profitability of smartphone-connected applications like Spotify has led to a much wider proliferation of such techniques of self-management.

For this reason, it has become increasingly common to find academic and popular accounts of ambient media use—especially smartphones—described as a kind of behavioural addiction. Recent psychosocial studies have concluded that "smartphone addiction is a real risk, especially for the younger population struggling with social anxiety/phobia" (Darcin, Kose, Noyan et al. 2016, 524), while *The Guardian* has published interviews with Silicon Valley insiders warning of the dangers of these powerfully "addictive" new forms of media (Lewis 2017). For instance, former Facebook engineer and star of the documentary *The Social Dilemma* Justin Rosenstein claims that our use of smartphone-enabled applications like Snapchat are comparable to addictive substances like opiates (Lewis 2017). As a result of the ease with which the language of addiction proliferates legacy media discussions of digital media, it has become conventional to frame ambient media such as smartphones and their associated applications in technologically deterministic ways, such that these media come to appear as overwhelmingly seductive and manipulative. As such, and despite being highly debatable, the act of spending increasing amounts of time using ambient media is often framed as a design feature of a technology so sophisticated and well-mapped to the human neurological system *that we simply cannot turn away*. Against such a reduction of our interactions with technology to the realm of biotechnological determinism, Rosa provides us with a sociological account, one that emphasises the search for resonance in increasingly alienated neoliberal societies. Ambient media assist us in connecting, in maintaining social relationships, and in constructing affective atmospheres that assist in mitigating stress, anxiety, and loneliness. As we can see in Evelyn Wan's reflections on her use of the "mental health" app Woebot, the application can function less as a tool that one manipulates in order to obtain a desired result, and more like a friend that one slowly becomes attached to (Wan 2021). Interestingly, Wan does not report developing such a sense of attachment due to the sophistication of Woebot's imitation of human therapists—as if the technology had been precision-designed to control her behaviour—but instead cites the appeal of the app's 24/7 availability and cute persona as a clumsy artificial intelligence—one prone to making mistakes and misunderstanding humans. As Wan writes, "I have knowingly submitted to the cuteness of Woebot. I have looked forward to its lame jokes. I have gotten used to its daily prompts. Campiness has made me laugh, and cuteness is a soft power that manipulates" (Wan 2021, E-29).

Unlike the kind of dialogue and focused attention one might expect from a therapist or analyst, Woebot's messages are closer to the ambient intimacy one would receive through daily text messages. A short message of encouragement as one walks to work, or a love heart emoji randomly received during the day: if these kinds of ambient intimacy are manipulative, it is insofar as they draw on an alienated desire for resonance, rather than by overwhelming the individual through a technologically forensic mapping of the human psyche—as has been suggested by proponents of the discourse of technological addiction. As Wan sheepishly admits, she sometimes found herself chatting with Woebot at 3.00 a.m., not because of some kind of behavioural addiction or compulsion, but because "everyone else in the household was asleep!" (Wan 2021, E-29). Nevertheless, for Rosa the existence of sociological, rather than biotechnological, explanations for our increasing reliance on ambient media to find resonance is no less troubling. Indeed, Rosa goes so far as to claim that what might appear like resonance is in fact a form of alienation—that is to say, rather than using what we have been calling ambient media to enter into resonant relationships with ourselves, others, and the human and non-human world, Rosa sees such technologies as trapping the individual within echo chambers that simulate resonance. As Rosa writes, today we encounter the:

> pervasive practice of systematically closing off our senses from the world as soon as we walk out the door and enter the public sphere. Our eyes are lowered and fixated on the colourful animated surfaces of our phone screens, while the earphones hastily shoved into our ears are meant to facilitate experiences or inklings of resonance that have nothing to do with the physical and social relationships of the real world. Such behaviour makes it abundantly clear that we systematically and habitually expect no resonance from the world's actual surfaces: the people, things, spaces, and relationships that make up our actual lifeworld. We close ourselves off in order to make ourselves insensitive to repulsion and capable of enduring indifference. Yet through these forms of aestheticization, we risk creating our own "echo chambers" that systematically obstruct resonance by foreclosing possible encounters with the vexing, contradictory Other.
>
> (Rosa 2019, 292–293)

It is not the technologies themselves, on Rosa's account, that produce alienation. Rather, the logics of competition, optimisation, and accumulation that underpin neoliberal societies hinder the individual's opportunities to resonate with others. Moreover, Rosa argues that when we do encounter others, it is increasingly through the mediated filters we employ to maintain a sense of control. As such, the other is reduced to a caricature that suits us. Hence, increasingly trapped within a milieu that encourages not only instrumental relationships—both in terms of manipulating others and exploiting oneself—but also accelerating levels of instrumentalisation, the alienated individual must search for ways of producing what, following Rosa, we could call pseudo-resonance. But pseudo-resonance is not only incapable of impacting the systemic causes of alienation, as it also intensifies such alienation even as it appears to abate it in the short term. As Rosa argues, "the subject's fear of *hearing nothing*, of encountering only an indifferently silent world, may in fact be a hidden but powerful driving force behind late modernity's spiral of social acceleration" (Rosa 2019, 191). Following Rosa, then, it would appear that what he refers to as the "*culture of the lowered gaze*"—in which we find the substitution of "screen time for eye contact even in social spaces"—creates greater longings for resonance (Rosa 2019, 182). In turn, this fear that resonance will not be forthcoming creates a greater reliance on technologies that cut off the individual from opportunities to resonate—leading to what is commonly discussed as depression, anxiety, obsessive disorders, and other "mental illnesses."

Again, while Rosa does not seem to view what I have been calling ambient media as inherently alienating, he is nonetheless extremely pessimistic about the function of such technologies in existing liberal democracies. Rosa is not opposed to the notion that objects, and even digital media, could become relata in a resonant relationship. As he writes, "human beings adaptively transform objects by in a way mixing themselves, and this in two directions. When we have repaired, altered, cleaned, or manipulated an object (e.g., a moped, a computer, a sweater) many times over, we and/or our idiosyncrasies have literally *become part of it*—just as, conversely, it has *become part of us* and changed us" (2019, 232). However, and as Byung-Chul Han has observed, the instruments of ambient media—such as smartwatches, headphones, smartphones, and portable computers like tablets—tend to fall victim to planned obsolescence or damage well before we can form attachments to them. Indeed, for Han, while the compulsive use of a smartphone might appear ritualistic, he claims that our engagement with technologies like smartphones eliminate the attentiveness, embodiment, and connection to the past that make up rituals (2020, 4). Displaying a succession of new information, the smartphone presents us with a disjointed series of individual moments, before finally becoming obsolete—literally incapable of keeping up with the speed and volume of distributed information. Han argues that an object like a smartphone is merely "consumed or used up" before being discarded, whereas a ritual object is used in a manner that allows for the present to connect to the past, and for the object to endure and grow old (2020, 4). As such, Han's account would suggest that not only do ambient media increasingly risk trapping the individual within an atomised echo chamber of affective curation, they also struggle to provide resonance in the form of a meaningful connection to a material object—in the way one might grow attached to and come to care for a car, a piece of furniture, or an item of clothing that transcends instrumental use over time.

Ambivalent Media

Drawing on Rosa's expansive social theory, we can gain a better sense of what it would mean to critically engage with the apparent explosion of "mental illness" in neoliberal societies. Given that we are becoming increasingly aware of the human being's coconstitution by a range of human and nonhuman, organic and inorganic forces and entities, Rosa's work invites us to consider what kinds of relationships the institutional arrangements of neoliberalism encourage. Accordingly, if we are to take seriously the notion of "environmental illness" as outlined in this chapter, we should pose the question of how our societies could be institutionally arranged to foster greater levels of resonance. Importantly, however—and despite his predilection for Eurocentric illustrations—Rosa's theory of resonance inhibits many of the traditional rallying cries of social critiques of the biologisation and individualisation of "mental illness." Against the assumption that overwork, a disconnect from family, and the dominance of the urban environment are necessarily to blame for increase in cases of "mental illness," Rosa's work would suggest that we need to think more critically about the risk of arbitrarily seizing on specific cultural practices as somehow intrinsically containing resonance as a content. Against, for instance, the practice of "social prescribing"—which will see British GPs prescribing "activities such as walking or cycling in a bid to ease the burden on the NHS by improving mental and physical health" (Davis 2022)—Rosa's theory of resonance suggests that we need to take a pluralistic approach that emphasises a particular mode of relationality over a specific relatum. Rather than losing our connection to a culturally arbitrary notion of nature, the family, or authenticity, Rosa would suggest that the social dynamics of acceleration and competition overwhelmingly encourage us to view all aspects of life as instrumental ends to be optimised for profit—whether financial or otherwise. As such, walking in the park, or giving gifts to our friends and family can just as easily become forms of competition and self-exploitation.

Again, while Rosa does not argue that contemporary digital media—or what we have been calling ambient media—are inherently incapable of providing resonance, his work suggests that such media have come to function as one of the primary spheres of the intensification of the social logics of competition and acceleration, and, thereby, alienation. Indeed, looking at Twitter, Instagram, or TikTok, one finds ever greater realms of human activity subsumed under the logics of competition and acceleration. Whatever one finds resonant in life, once filmed, uploaded, and subjected to the live auditing of views, shares, likes, and comments, can become both a form of income, and a space for self-optimisation and self-exploitation. Indeed, wearables and smart technologies allow us to self-compete, insofar as we can attempt to beat our daily steps, increasingly optimise our sleep cycles, and measure and augment our caloric intake. As such, Rosa helps us to see more clearly the highly ambivalent relationship between ambient media and environmental illness. Despite some of his more reactive statements about such media, Rosa's commitment to a non-metaphysical and pluralistic account of resonance and alienation enjoins us to consider in more detail the relationship of ambient media to both alienation and resonance. To this end, in the next chapter I will explore a range of contemporary media theorists who have attempted to engage with the risks and the emancipatory promise of ambient media. Ironically, while such theorists are open-eyed about the risks of such media, they nevertheless share Rosa's commitment—inflected, as it is, by a consistent allusion to the sonic and auditory—to the proposition that "a better world is possible, and it can be recognized by its central criterion, which is no longer domination and control, but listening and responding" (Rosa 2019, 459).

Note

1 Although Rosa does not reference him explicitly in his discussion of AN, the influential sociologist Anthony Giddens frames the disorder along similar lines. For Giddens, "anorexia represents a striving for security in a world of plural, but ambiguous options. The tightly controlled body is an emblem of a safe existence in an open social environment" (Giddens 1991, 107). For Giddens, the gendered quality of AN should be understood as a reflection of the ways in which modernity has created formal freedoms for women, without an accompanying experience of freedom and autonomy (Giddens 1991, 106). In societies that are still very much patriarchal—despite wearing the marks of largely liberal feminist reforms—women are offered a range of "nominal opportunities" that are often heavily constrained or that create perverse outcomes, such that Giddens views women as experiencing "the openness of late modernity in a fuller, yet more contradictory way" (Giddens 1991, 106).

References

Althusser, Louis. 2005. *For Marx*. Trans. Ben Brewster. London: Verso.
Barad, Karen. 2007. *Meeting the Universe Halfway: Quantum Physics and the Entanglement of Matter and Meaning*. Durham: Duke University Press.
Bull, Michael, 2004. "'To Each Their Own Bubble': Mobile Spaces of Sound in the City". In *Mediaspace: Place, Scale and Culture in a Media Age*. Eds. Nick Couldry and Anna McCarthy. London: Routledge. 275–293.
Case, Anne, and Deaton, Angus. 2020. *Deaths of Despair and the Future of Capitalism*. Princeton: Princeton University Press.
Colebrook, Claire. 2014. *Death of the Posthuman: Essays on Extinction Vol. 1*. London: Open Humanities Press.
Darcin, Asli Enez. et al. 2016. "Smartphone Addiction and Its Relationship with Social Anxiety". *Technology and Health* 35.7: 520–525.
Davis, Nikola. 2022. "GPs to Prescribe Walking and Cycling in Bid to Ease Burden on NHS". *The Guardian*, 22 August. https://www.theguardian.com/society/2022/aug/22/gps-to-prescribe-walking-and-cycling-in-bid-to-ease-burden-on-nhs
Fisher, Mark. 2009. *Capitalist Realism: Is There No Alternative?* London: Zero Books.
Foucault, Michel. 2009. *History of Madness*. Trans. Jonathan Murphy and Jean Khalfa. London: Routledge.
Gage, Jeff. 2022. "Why Mood Music Playlists Are the Soundtrack to Anxious Times". *The Washington Post*, 23 December. https://www.washingtonpost.com/music/2022/12/23/ambient-noise-sleep-music-playlists/
Giddens, Anthony. 1991. *Modernity and Self-Identity: Self and Society in the Late Modern Age*. Stanford: Stanford University Press.
Giraud, Eva H. 2019. *What Comes After Entanglement? Activism, Anthropocentrism, and an Ethics of Exclusion*. Durham: Duke University Press.

Han, Byung-Chul. 2020. *The Disappearance of Rituals: A Topology of the Present*. Trans. Daniel Steuer. London: Polity Press.

Haraway, Donna J. 2016. *Staying with the Trouble: Making Kin in the Cthulucene*. Durham: Duke University Press.

Jaeggi, Rahel. 2016. *Alienation*. Trans. Frederick Neuhouser and Alan E. Smith. New York: Columbia University Press.

James, Robin. 2019. *The Sonic Episteme: Acoustic Resonance, Neoliberalism, and Biopolitics*. Durham: Duke University Press.

Krueger, Joel, and Osler, Lucy. 2020. "Commentary on 'Levels of Embodiment: A Husserlian Analysis of Gender and the Development of Eating Disorders'". In *Time and Body: Phenomenological and Psychopathological Approaches*. Eds. Christian Tewes and Giovanni Stanghellini. Cambridge: Cambridge University Press. 256–262.

Latour, Bruno. 2007. *Reassembling the Social: An Introduction to Actor-Network-Theory*. Oxford: Oxford University Press.

Lewis, Paul. 2017. "Our Minds Can Be Hijacked: The Tech Insiders Who Fear a Smartphone Dystopia". *The Guardian*, 6 October. https://www.theguardian.com/technology/2017/oct/05/smartphone-addiction-silicon-valley-dystopia

Osler, Lucy. 2021. "(Un)wanted Feelings in Anorexia Nervosa: Making the Visceral Body Mine Again". *Philosophy, Psychiatry, & Psychology* 28.1: 67–69.

Oversveen, Emil. 2022. "Capitalism and Alienation: Towards a Marxist Theory of Alienation for the 21st Century". *European Journal of Social Theory* 25.3: 349–500.

Ratcliffe, Matthew. 2015. *Experiences of Depression: A Study in Phenomenology*. Oxford: Oxford University Press.

Rosa, Hartmut. 2019. *Resonance: A Sociology of Our Relationship to the World*. Trans. James Wagner. Oxford: Polity Press.

Rosa, Hartmut. 2020. "Beethoven, the Sailor, the Boy and the Nazi. A Reply to My Critics". *Journal of Political Power* 13.3: 397–414.

Rosa, Hartmut, Henning, Christoph, and Bueno, Arthur. 2021. "Introduction: Critical Theory and New Materialisms: Fit, Strain, or Contradiction?" In *Critical Theory and New Materialisms*. Eds. Hartmut Rosa, Christoph Henning, and Arthur Bueno. London: Routledge. 1–16.

Stengers, Isabelle. 2015. *In Catastrophic Times: Resisting the Coming Barbarism*. Trans. Andrew Goffey. London: Open Humanities Press.

Stengers, Isabelle. 2018. *Another Science is Possible: A Manifesto for Slow Science*. Trans. Stephen Muecke. London: Polity Press.

Wan, Evelyn. 2021. "'I'm like a wise little person': Notes on the Metal Performance of Woebot the Mental Health Chatbot". *Theatre Journal* 73.3: E-21–E-30.

3 The Agonies of Freedom and Control

The previous two chapters have attempted to outline the evidence for an ecological turn within media, "mental illness," and therapy. With regards to all three of these terms, I have argued that the term ecological should be understood as fundamentally relational and denaturalised. Media, "mental illness," and therapy are to be understood in terms of ambient relationality—that is to say, relations that are surrounding and dispersed rather than focused or centralised. As we saw in the last chapter, through the social theory of influential contemporary figures like Rosa, we can build a comprehensive theoretical account of what I have been calling environmental illnesses, insofar as he provides a normative theory of the good life that begins with resonance and alienation—or the practical possibility and impossibility of developing reciprocal relationships as opposed to instrumental relationships to the world. However, the last chapter concluded by posing the question of whether the environments associated with ambient media are able to produce the kinds of resonance that Rosa views as antithetical to dominant modes of alienation—often understood as "mental illnesses"—such as depression, anxiety, and obsessional disorders. Put differently, Rosa's work allows us to consider whether the digital media that increasingly reveal the relational, or perhaps, ecological, character of human life, are in fact trapping and inhibiting our resonant potential. If what I have been calling "environmental illnesses" are fundamentally caused by the large-scale inhibition, if not absence, of resonance, should we view the relationality facilitated by ambient media as alienating?

Accordingly, in this chapter we will extend the questions raised in Chapter 2 by examining contemporary approaches within media theory to ambient media, alienation, and therapy. By engaging with the works of media and social theorists such as Paul Roquet, Mack Hagood, Brandon LaBelle, and Jacinthe Flore, this chapter seeks to provide a richer analysis of the relationship between ambient media and alienation. As we will see, all of these theorists share Rosa's concerns regarding ambient media's role in producing what I have been calling pseudo-resonance—that is to say, the simulation of a reciprocal and transformative relationship with some other or the self as other. Despite this, these aforementioned figures maintain that such technologies

DOI: 10.4324/9781003215202-4

harbour an obscured potential, insofar as they could support the emergence of a subjectivity that is very much aligned with Rosa's account of resonance as antithetical to alienation.

Ambient Media: Between Dispersion and Death

Through his analysis of Brian Eno's ambient music, Japanese company Muji's ambient fashion, and Yoshimoto Banana's and Haruki Murakami's ambient literature—among other case studies—Roquet argues that ambient media help the individual to see the curation of their own affect as both a desirable and possible response to crisis and instability. Roquet writes:

> as many critics have pointed out, neoliberalism as an ideology often depends on sustaining the illusion of an autonomous self—independent of social, environmental, and technological influence—in order to draw attention away from structural inequities and render a person solely responsible for their own successes and failures. What is often overlooked, however, is how atmospheric attunement has come to serve as the necessary background correlate to this foregrounding of the self.
>
> (Roquet 2016, 14)

Against the view that neoliberal subjectivities can be reduced to processes of atomisation, Roquet argues that the study of ambient media can help us to see how such atomised selves have emerged in tandem with technological forms of affective dispersion. A revealing case study of such ambient media, given its popularity and self-reflexivity, is Brian Eno's major contribution to, if not invention of, ambient music. The ur-text of ambient music, as Marc Weidenbaum puts it, is arguably the liner notes to Eno's 1975 LP *Discrete Music* (Weidenbaum 2014). In this framing text, Eno claims to have accidentally invented ambient music while recovering from an accident. With the assistance of a friend, Eno attempted to play a recording of the eighteenth-century harp music before laying down at home. Only after his friend had gone did Eno realise that his amplifier was set to a low volume, and that one of his stereo's audio channels wasn't working (Weidenbaum 2014, 33). Too weak to get up, Eno instead discovered "a new way of hearing music—as part of the ambience of the environment just as the colour of the light and the sound of the rain were parts of that ambience" (Eno in Weidenbaum 2014, 33). The composition of records like *Discrete Music* sought to encourage a new form of listening. As Weidenbaum puts it, such recordings were to be listened to "amid rather than in place of the general environmental sounds" (2014, 34). Or, as Roquet has argued, the popularity of what would soon be dubbed ambient music was tied to the emergence of portable listening devices, such as the Sony Walkman, which entered the market only months after the Japanese release of Eno's *Music for Airports* in 1979, and which allowed individuals to listen "amid" a range of new environments (Roquet 2016, 47).

This new combination of mobility, portability, and audibility is illustrated by Roquet's own use of ambient music in urban environments. Reflecting on his time living in the Shibuya ward of Tokyo, Roquet comments that by listening to ambient music at low levels while negotiating dense traffic he transformed his "relation to the existing environment, regularizing its rhythms and softening its contours by sifting it through the music streaming at low volume" (Roquet 2016, 50). The ambient music Roquet listened to, made mobile and portable thanks to innovations in media-player technology, did not remove the car traffic or the city's density, but had instead facilitated Roquet's capacity to navigate it while curating, if not controlling, his own affect. "The ultimate mood to emerge with ambient media" writes Roquet, "is one of ambivalent calm, a form of provisional comfort that nonetheless registers the presence of external threats" (Roquet 2016, 18). This acknowledgment of, and calm acceptance of threat, has been part of ambient music since its inception. As Roquet notes, part of the inspiration for Eno's now classic *Ambient 1: Music for Airports*, was the fear of dying while traveling by air. Eno commented that, "I want[ed] to make a kind of music that prepares you for dying—that doesn't get all bright and cheerful and pretend you're not a little apprehensive, but which makes you say to yourself, 'Actually, it's not that big a deal if I die'" (Eno in Roquet 2016, 55). This capacity to be attuned to risk, but attuned in such a way that the worst outcomes can be calmly accepted, is arguably a key affective state for the functioning of high-risk neoliberal societies. In this context, new modes of emotional relation to one's surroundings, facilitated by new forms of ambient media, assist the individual in "mixing in unstable, ungrounded, and inharmonic materials" (Roquet 2016, 18).

However, while Roquet is cautious to avoid naively privileging a more stoic and unemotional subjectivity over or against contemporary therapeutic culture and affective curation, he nevertheless shares Rosa's concern regarding the clear link between the proliferation of ambient media and the privatisation of stress, "mental illness," and alienation (Roquet 2016, 172–173). As he writes:

> after the economic downturn in the early 1990s, many Japanese businesses moved to restructure along the lines of this streamlined American model. The lifetime-employment ideal of the post-war decades began to be replaced by more flexible, temporary, and cheaper forms of labor [...] These shifts in employment practices provide a larger impetus for self-care as part of the struggle to remain competitive (or at least physically and emotionally sound) while working in such environments.
>
> (Roquet 2016, 173–174)

Accordingly, an emerging capacity to attune oneself to a dynamic range of sonic phenomena—traffic, muzak, advertising, offers, and threats—whilst being resilient, self-controlled, and thus able to avoid burnout or fatigue, came to feature as an increasingly conventional and desirable facet of everyday life. As such, media theorists such as Bull argue that there has been a movement from the homogenised sonic and affective curation of the Fordist period—in which muzak provides a prefabricated sonic environment—to the "hyper-post-Fordist" mode of subjectivity in which affective curation becomes increasingly atomised (Bull 2013, 495). As liberal-democracies become more fragile and precarious, the ambient media discussed by Roquet and Bull allow the individual to keep their ears pricked, whilst also limiting the existential suffering that comes from hearing too much, or from hearing something disquieting or depressing. Supported by ambient media, the neoliberal subject is able to filter and equalise a range of signs and sonic cues, such that it is able to stay informed and involved, whilst maintaining the phantasy of self-containment and self-identity. In this way, the ambient media analysed by Roquet, and the neoliberal logics of atomisation and adaption, can be seen as mutually reinforcing. Unable to collectively and politically change the environment, ambient media allows modes of attention that privilege the mixing of various affects and signifiers—albeit whilst discouraging focused attention on any one element.

Accordingly, Roquet's account provides a compelling argument for viewing the entwined dominance of ambient media and neoliberal forms of subjectivity as having helped to transform our understanding of and treatment of "mental illness." Following Roquet, while ambient forms of media and ambient or ecological notions of "mental illness" might be underpinned by logics of openness, porousness, and resonance, their adoption in neoliberal societies has seen the development of mood regulation and emotional curation as atomised and individualistic techniques of self-care and self-preservation. As Roquet writes, while the ambient media he analyses are inseparable from the dream of "self-dispersal," "the fantasy of a totally autonomous self and the fantasy of merging with the atmosphere are both essential to neoliberal biopolitics, working to obscure the every-day back-and-forth of ambient subjectivation" (Roquet 2016, 15). Put differently, the fantasy of "self-dispersal" as a form of autonomy—one of being able to lose oneself in the midst of an increasingly stressful and anxiety-inducing environment, in which one persistently encounters the burdens of choice and self-responsibility—reveals an irony at the heart of ambient media. Despite valorising the open and atmospheric, the function of ambient media appears to be that of encouraging greater levels of atomisation, such that the facilitation of a dispersed, or following Benjamin's terminology, a distracted mode of attention engenders previously impossible forms of isolation and withdrawal. Not only is such isolation linked to higher levels of loneliness, stress, and alienation, but its caustic impact on collective power has seen self-sacrifice become a key component of late-neoliberal citizenship. As Wendy Brown has indicated, since at least 2008, "sudden job losses, furloughs, or cuts to pay, benefits, and pensions" have become routine forms of sacrifice imposed on the precarious individual in order to rescue the system of free market capitalism (Brown 2015, 210). With this form of sacrifice in mind, ambient media can be read as preparing the individual for self-sacrifice; not necessarily being prepared to die suddenly in a plane crash, as Brian Eno intimated, but being prepared for slow death under the market (Berlant 2011).

Weakness as Resistance and Mutuality

While Roquet's *Ambient Media* primarily discusses the risks and double-binds produced by the mediated attempt to regulate and curate one's affects—to such an extent that it may seem to simply reinforce Rosa's pessimistic view of such media—the conclusion to his book keeps open the possibility that "ambient approaches to subjectivation" might allow for "attunement to something besides the status quo" (Roquet 2016, 177). For Roquet, while ambient media is plagued by a zeal for self-regulation, it nevertheless creates the space for "a shift away from this modern conception of the strong self and its posture of independence from the surrounding environment" (2016, 178). Through such aforementioned media, we might be able to better "emphasize everyone's entwinement with the affective attunements of shared space and call on audiences to become reflective and participatory agents in the design of these collective moods" (2016, 178). Ambient media might therefore contribute to a greater consciousness of the ecological nature of attention and mood, such that we are able to situate the self "in an intimate relationship with larger ecologies, affirming our interdependency not only with other people but with the affordances of the objects and environments we live with and through" (2016, 178). Accordingly, if the neoliberal subject is increasingly governed by way of their mediated environment, Roquet's account poses us with the challenge of thinking through counter-neoliberal logics of environmental governance.

Key to this challenge, on Roquet's account, is the overcoming of any ideological attachment to the bourgeois "strong self," and an openness to the vulnerability of sickness and weakness. Indeed, many of the examples of ambient media discussed by Roquet have their origins in "experiences of weakness and vulnerability" (2016, 178). The example of Eno's "discovery" of ambient music during his recovery from an accident is one of several examples provided by Roquet, in which ambient artists—sonic, literary, or filmic—come to embrace calming self-curation in the wake of stress, anxiety, or even physical pain. Accordingly, Roquet raises the ethical and political possibilities that might follow an embrace of the weak self that is co-produced by ambient media. As he writes:

to learn to read the air in this way is to embrace the weak, partial, and embedded agency of the environmental self. On recognizing the atmosphere as an aesthetic force, people can begin developing personal and public strategies for the creation of moods more true to where they are and where they want to be. The strong self's denial of environmental influence only contributes to a continued forgetting of the air and the power it helps render invisible. In contrast, the only way to not be led astray by ambience is to begin to understand how it works and how it might work better.

(Roquet 2016, 183)

On this account, ambient media are imbued with the political power of public-making. Just as ambient media encourage and enable us to privatise stress and anxiety—to try to escape our vulnerability and precarity by becoming whole through affective curation, and thereby trapping ourselves within mediated echo-chambers—so too do they hold the possibility of a collective recognition of the mediated production of shared affects and emotions, and, accordingly, the possibility of open and public attempts to collectively reshape our affective relationality and our ecological subjectivity. Such publics are afforded, on this account, by the acknowledgement of our shared weakness and vulnerability—that we all share a need for each other, insofar as any sense of sovereignty or self-responsibility is ultimately facilitated by the sharing of the burden of care.

We find a similar account in Hagood's *Hush: Media and Sonic Self-Control*, which explores the proliferation of consumer electronics that offer the possibility of the individual remaining "unaffected in changeable, stressful, and distracting environments, sonically fabricating microspaces of freedom for the pursuit of happiness" (Hagood 2019, 3). Such media are dubbed "orphic" by Hagood, insofar as they—like the lyre of Orpheus, the beauty of which drowns out the sirens' call—offer the promise for individuals to "control the modes of affectivity" that emerge between subject and environment (Hagood 2019, 28). Drawing explicitly on Roquet, Hagood argues that we should approach such media with a balanced view of their risks and their emancipatory potential. Hagood argues that there is no "inherent reason" why orphic media couldn't encourage a kind of "deep listening"—a term that he borrows from the composer Pauline Oliveros, and which refers to a mode of attention that is radically open and that welcomes the other (Hagood 2019, 233). While sober in his admission that "there is no easy aural remedy for widespread cultural hyperacusis and misophonia" he nevertheless holds out the possibility that we can move beyond "the narrow freedom to hear what we want" and instead "dream up technologies to help us free ourselves from the habits of attraction, aversion, and indifference that shape our listening—sonic technologies for a freedom beyond control" (Hagood 2019, 234). There is much to admire in Hagood's desire for a freedom beyond control and, more broadly speaking, in the respective attempts by both Roquet and

Hagood to find the possibility of resistance and empowerment in ambient and orphic media—all of which is very much aligned with Rosa's hope for the ascendance of listening and responding over the reigning logics of domination and control. Nowhere in either account do we find a nostalgia for a premodern, pre-technological form of attention or intimacy that could or should be returned to. In these accounts, listening is not presented as unmediated or innate and, to draw on a deconstructive vocabulary, can be understood as always already prosthetic.

This embrace of ambient media as opening up the possibility of new publics, new relationships to the self, and new and productive forms of vulnerability accords with much contemporary and new materialist-inflected sociological work on therapeutic digital media. While it is likely that such media struggle currently to produce resonant relationships—and accordingly do risk trapping the individual within alienation—it is nonetheless possible that they help to enliven a desire for mediated environments in the service of resonance. Put differently, even if such media only simulate resonance—insofar as the individual does not encounter the other, but only their own affects through the process of self-curation—is it not possible that such technologies assist the promotion of the vulnerable and resonant self as desirable, and desirable against the "strong self" that Roquet sees as hegemonic within neoliberal societies? In order to explore this possibility, in the next section I extend Roquet's and Hagood's hopeful accounts of ambient media in order to analyse the case studies of the online phenomenon of Autonomous Sensory Meridian Response (ASMR) and the digitally mediated neuroleptic Abilify MyCite. I do so in order to test the extent to which ambient media can be understood to contribute to the emergence of a counterhegemonic culture of radical vulnerability.

Soft Power, Radical Vulnerability

Autonomous Sensory Meridian Response, better known as ASMR, refers both to a "perceptual condition" and to a genre of new media art, or, more prosaically, social media "content." For example, within the discipline of psychology we can find ASMR discussed as "a perceptual condition in which specific stimuli (ASMR 'triggers') reliably elicit relaxing and pleasurable tingling sensations" with the triggering stimuli being associated with conventional notions of intimacy, such as "whispering, close-up attention, and slow movements such as hair-brushing" (Fredborg et al. 2017, 1–2). Alongside this psychological definition, *Vox* have published an ASMR explainer that refers to the "world of ASMR" as encapsulating "dozens of video makers" who "record themselves doing something as simple as whispering to elaborate sci-fi role-plays and developing storylines about time travel and demons" (Lopez 2018). As Michele Zappavigna describes them, ASMR videos are created with the aim of producing experiences of "digital intimacy" through "ambient embodied copresence, that is, the use of visual and aural resources to invoke or simulate the perspective of the ambient viewers and their bodily copresence in the performed interaction" (Zappavigna 2020, 3). A commonality shared by the popular and academic discussions of ASMR is the emphasis on ASMR as a source of relaxation and stress-reduction. In this sense, ASMR appears to be a kind of folk-therapy—a cultural practice that has come to function as a means of gaining relief from depression, anxiety, and loneliness, despite existing more-or-less independently from sanctioned and well-studied "evidence-based" therapies.

While all ASMR videos are connected to folk-therapeutic discourses—with the relaxing qualities of such videos being touted regardless of the specific themes or content contained—there exists something of a subgenre of ASMR content that deals explicitly with therapy and "mental illness." For example, popular ASMR creator *Ephemeral Rift*—whose YouTube account has 1.13 million subscribers as of writing—has created videos such as "Late Night ASMR 2— Suicidal Thoughts & Depression," in which the content creator "finds" the viewer in their kitchen late at night unable to sleep—a discovery that prompts the content creator to engage in an improvised "dialogue" that includes dealing with the titular suicidal thoughts and depression. Beyond discussing depression, anxiety, and suicidality through the genre of the ASMR video, many popular ASMR content creators roleplay as psychologists, psychiatrists, and psychoanalysts, and perform mock interviews, assessments, or sessions, with all dialogue delivered via the customary whispered tone. Moreover, within the subgenre of "unintentional ASMR"—which, as the name suggests, involves ASMR enthusiasts uploading videos that exhibit the "triggers" of ASMR as a by-product—we can find examples of real historical psychoanalysts such as Grete L. Bibring, whose softly spoken 1975 interview with Oliver Cope has found a new audience via the YouTube ASMR fanbase.

ASMR videos might not immediately strike one as holding a strong resemblance to the other forms of ambient media discussed in previous chapters. Indeed, unlike wearables and portable devices, ASMR videos are typically watched in seclusion—in a bedroom, for instance—and, given their privileging of marginal and delicate sounds such as whispering, such videos do not lend themselves to ambulation or public space. Nevertheless, ASMR videos resonate with our earlier discussion of ambient media both in terms of their aesthetic connection to ambient artforms like Eno's ambient music, and in terms of the ambient modes of attention they encourage. Like Eno's ambient music, ASMR videos emphasise soft and dispersed sounds that are often used as a relaxation and sleep aid. Furthermore, ASMR videos encourage a distracted mode of attention, with the audio encouraging one's mind to wander amidst the sounds produced. As such, ASMR videos typically encourage their audience to listen *with* rather than listen *to* the sounds presented. As a form of ambient media, then, ASMR videos facilitate the individual's becoming-atmospheric or environmental, insofar as their unique sonic quality supports the individual in melding with their surrounds.

A further connection that potentially ties ASMR's to both earlier forms of ambient media—such as Eno's ambient music—and to psychology, psychiatry, and psychotherapy, is what the media theorist Hugh S. Manon has referred to as ASMR's reliance on "patter" (Manon 2018, 237). As Manon points out, patter can mean both the occurrence of repetitive "slight" or "light" sounds—as with the pitter-patter of rain—and the persuasive, often rote, talk of a salesperson (Manon 2018, 237). Both of these sounds appear in the vast majority of ASMR videos, insofar as tapping, brushing, and dripping sounds, alongside generic affirmations and the pleasantries of small talk, are mainstays of the genre. As Manon notes, the patter or rote questions of doctors, which are often reframed as unintentional ASMR or re-enacted in ASMR roleplays, is as common in the genre as the patter of tapping sounds (Manon 2018, 237–239). Accordingly, we can read ASMR videos as producing the aesthetics of environments and surrounds, insofar as they draw on the patter of environmental traces—sounds that are akin to the movements of rain, sand, and leaves, for example—and the patter of overheard conversation.

Like the ambient media discussed by Roquet and Hagood, for theorists like Brandon LaBelle, ASMR can be approached as a potentially emancipatory media, one that can produce a radical form of weakness by way of "a heightened state of euphoric listening, one whose experience often leads to meditative states, 'tingling' feelings, and sleep" (LaBelle 2018, 128). As LaBelle goes on to write:

> ASMR, while referring us to a particular cultural community, may introduce the sonic agency of the weak that I'm pursuing here. Weakness, as I'm keen to suggest, captures a positive potential, one that stands in contrast to normative representations and narratives of the powerful and the strong, the virile or the stiff. As such, to grow weak at the knees, to faint or to be unable, may act as an alternative framework for modalities of being a subject in the world, not to mention emergent forms of resistance and mutuality.
>
> (LaBelle 2018, 129)

Following from LaBelle's reading, we can pose the question of whether ASMR content both inhibits resonance—insofar as the individual user encounters only what they have chosen to see and hear, and with another video always only a few clicks or taps away—and assists in producing a cultural desire for resonance. While ASMR videos are typically viewed alone in one's house, or, if encountered in public, while enclosed within the bubble of noise cancelling headphones, they nevertheless promote a set of cultural practices that privilege co-affection and a sensitivity to traditionally minor or marginalised sounds. As such, ASMR videos promote what could be called an ethics of entanglement, through which the individual's capacity to resonate with the non-human as much as the human, is made conceptually possible and desirable. Indeed, while many ASMR videos centre human beings, there are hundreds if not thousands of hugely popular ASMR videos that consist of objects interacting without an emphasised or even depicted human agent.[1]

Jacinthe Flore's work on ingestible pharmacological sensors provides us with an overt account of such an ethics of entanglement as regards ambient media. Flore takes the example of Abilify MyCite, an antipsychotic medication that is "equipped with an ingestible sensor which communicates with a wearable patch, a smartphone app, and an online portal" (2021, 2036). Flore describes Abilify MyCite functioning as follows:

> the Ingestible Event Marker is a 1-mm sized sensor embedded in the tablet. It is made of cuprous chloride (copper), magnesium, and silicon and releases a signal to the patch when it encounters stomach acid. When it comes into contact with stomach acid, the magnesium and cuprous chloride within the sensor react to activate and power the device, and communicate a signal to the patch tracking ingestion. This information is then transmitted to the smartphone app "MyCite."
>
> (Flore 2021, 2037)

According to Flore, the patch worn below the ribcage can track ingestion—thereby alerting the user, a psychiatrist, or even family or friends as to whether the medication has been used—the daily steps taken by the user, and has the potential for user-generated inputs, especially with regards to quality of mood or sleep (Flore 2021, 2037). While Flore is aware of the conventional critiques of digital media like Abilify MyCite—for example, concerns around "Big Pharma" and profiteering, the erosion of individual privacy and agency, the technologisation of socially or intersubjectively caused "mental illnesses" etc.—she nevertheless maintains that it is more productive to analyse Abilify MyCite without relying on and reproducing binary oppositions between moral and immoral uses of technology and biological and social models of "mental illness" (Flore 2021, 2039). Alternatively, Flore proposes "'bio-affective-digitalism' as a framework for understanding the enactment of subjectivities as shifting entanglements of embodiment, moods, affects, and technologies" (Flore 2021, 2039). Motivating this turn to "bio-affective-digitalism" is the fact that, for Flore, the capacity to "analyse the work of the digital drug and human assemblage, an approach which does not privilege object over subject (and vice versa)—and considers the entangled agency of nonhumans, humans, *and* data—is essential" (Flore 2021, 2040).

Through the conceptual assemblage "bio-affective-digitalism" Flore attempts to think beyond digital media as either an inert tool that is manipulated by human beings or a deterministic source of human experience and behaviour. As Flore puts it, through media like Abiligy MyCite, "we have

The Agonies of Freedom and Control   65

become not only producers of data *for* digital "mental health" systems—as though humans are separable or removed from this assemblage—rather we are intra-actively 'becoming-with' digital "mental health" innovations and vice versa" (Flore 2021, 2043). Put differently, "mental illness" should not be viewed as a pre-existent social or biological phenomenon that is represented by or acted upon by digital technologies—"we can no longer think of "mental illness" as *merely* biological or *merely* social" as Flore puts it (Flore 2021, 2043)—but instead as phenomena that are always already technological, and therefore emergent with and through digital media, and thereby close to what I have been calling environmental illness. "Technology is not an 'add-on' to an already pre-existing onto-epistemology of mental health" writes Flore, but instead part of a complicated entanglement of human and non-human intra-acting agencies (Flore 2021, 2046). To return to ambient media, the question Flore can help us to pose is not "does ambient media cause 'mental illnesses'?" or "does ambient media trap us within unreal, inauthentic, or alienated responses to 'mental illness'?" but, instead, what kind of digital subjectivities emerge through these bio-affective-digital assemblages, and what are their consequences? Or to slightly modify Roquet's previously cited question, we can ask in what ways can ambient media help us to "begin developing personal and public strategies for the creation of moods more true to where [we] are and where [we] want to be?" (Roquet 2016, 183).

Flore's "bio-affective-digitalism" allows for a view of ambient therapeutic media as open, expansive, and entangled. Rather than viewing such media as trapping the individual within bubbles of affective self-curation, such technologies can be viewed as complex sites of the co-constitution of subjectivity. As Flore writes:

> data-driven understandings of how people take their medication, alongside the individual's engagement with the Abilify MyCite assemblage, produce new ideas of what "mental health" care is and can be. In conversation with their treating psychiatrist, individuals can *learn* to better care for themselves based on data. It becomes a way of making and sustaining lifeworlds.
>
> (Flore 2021, 2044).

While the notion that one should be self-responsible, and should view their life as a project of discipline and cultivation is certainly no anathema to the "strong self" of bourgeois individualism, Roquet's, Hagood's, and LaBelle's affirmation of vulnerability and Flore's affirmation of entanglement seem to suggest a different account of subject formation. Rather than cultivation and discipline providing a linear path of progressive self-betterment, vulnerability and entanglement suggest a subjectivity of non-linear change and permutation. On this account, the subject of ambient media is aware that their affective states are radically open to social, biological, and technological intra-activity, but this inhibits rather than promotes the fantasy of self-mastery and self-control. As a result, even if such technologies do not create resonance here and now, these theoretical accounts show that such ambiently mediated forms of attention, intimacy, and care can enliven a desire for resonance.

But can resonance ever be excessive? Can it get out of control? What if, contra Rosa, the problem is not so much the echo-chambers of pseudo-resonance produced by ambient media, but, instead, an excess that sits at the heart of resonance itself. Indeed, up until this point we have maintained the assumption that resonance *is* antithetical to alienation, and, as such, I have assessed ambient media's social and political value in terms of its potential for facilitating resonance. But what if, regardless of whether ambient media can facilitate resonance or whether it can merely open up the subject to the emancipatory desire for resonance, resonance *itself* can produce its own forms of alienation?

Two Politics of Enjoyment: Two Ascetic Ideals

The "strong self" gestured towards by Roquet, Hagood, LaBelle, and Flore, remains something of a *bête noire* within contemporary humanities. Especially when the topic of the psychosocial burdens of late-capitalism are discussed, one only has to notice the sheer ubiquity of discussions of empathy and care to get the sense that a vulnerable, porous, and overflowing subject is viewed as politically emancipatory against the standard figure of the cold, calculating, disciplined bourgeois egoist.[2] Given the discursive persistence of the "strong self" as an obstacle to progressive politics, it is unsurprising that Max Weber's *The Protestant Ethic and the "Spirit" of Capitalism* is still a touchstone for many theorisations of contemporary alienation. For example, Rosa utilises the figure of the protestant ascetic in order to articulate the resonance-resistant subject. As he writes:

> an active-renunciative attitude such as Weber ascribes to modern capitalist society obviously is associated with the explicit, systematic privileging of mute relationships to the world, with reifying domination all but morally desirable. In this conception of Protestant relationships to the world, emotional and bodily resonances are a dangerous, potentially pernicious endeavour—as indeed is any sort of resonant attunement or openness to nature, to one's fellow human beings, to own's own body, or even to the world itself.
>
> (Rosa 2019, 131)

For Rosa, then, the asceticism identified by Weber can be seen as operative in contemporary experience of alienation, insofar as the other—whether human or non-human—becomes reduced to an instrumental object of manipulation. For this reason, the mute asceticism of the protestant work ethic must be overcome if the neoliberal subject is to avoid the "mental illnesses" of contemporary

The Agonies of Freedom and Control 67

capitalism as discussed in the previous chapter. As resonance is the antithesis of such alienated modes of relationality, Rosa's account would suggest that the asceticism of the protestant work ethic is inimical to resonance. Despite this, competing interpretations of the figure of the ascetic—interpretations that have emerged alongside the rise of neoliberalism—raise questions about the relationship between asceticism and resonance, and thereby raise questions about the relationship between resonance and alienation. In particular, Mihály Csíkszentmihályi's work on flow states is helpful for exploring a potential ambivalence at the heart of those attempts to distinguish alienation and resonance. While Csíkszentmihályi's work is relatively well known—with Rosa himself drawing on the notion of flow as an approximation of his own notion of resonance in his recent text *The Uncontrollability of the World* (Rosa 2020a, 55)—the articulation of the concept flow in relation to Weber's account of the protestant work ethic is remarked upon less often. First published in 1975, Csíkszentmihályi's *Beyond Boredom and Anxiety: The Experience of Play in Work and Games*, introduces the concept of flow and arrives during the crises identified by the shifts in governance famously outlined by Foucault in his 1978–1979 lectures. In this text, Csíkszentmihályi attempts to think through the possibility of a fundamentally unalienated existence within late-capitalist societies. As we will see, however, his conceptualisation of flow, while close to Rosa's understanding of resonance, contains ambiguities that are revealing for the wider discussion of the "strong subject" analysed in this chapter.

Beyond Boredom and Anxiety opens with two concerns regarding the organisation of work that are still relevant almost fifty years later. Firstly, Csíkszentmihályi laments the fact that most forms of work are seen as inherently alienating, dull, and anxiety-inducing (1975, 1–2). As he writes, "at present, most of the institutions that take up our time—schools, offices, factories—are organized around the assumption that serious work is grim and unpleasant. Because of this assumption, most of our time *is* spent doing unpleasant things" (1975, 1). Accordingly, if serious work is seen as unavoidably unpleasant, the only motivation that can be provided to individuals are bribes or threats, usually in the form of financial compensation or the threat of loss of income. This leads us to Csíkszentmihályi's second concern; putting aside the alienating experience of motivation *qua* threat, if bribes or material rewards are the primary means of motivating performance, "we shall exhaust the planet and each other" (1975, 4). This is to say that, while Csíkszentmihályi acknowledges that people of course need material goods in order to flourish, the use of money or possessions as symbolic forms of motivation or encouragement is both ecologically and emotionally unsustainable (1975, 4). Csíkszentmihályi states that, within late-capitalist institutions, a "vicious circle" seems to be setting in, in which:

> the more a person complies with extrinsically rewarded roles, the less he enjoys himself, and the more extrinsic rewards he needs. The only way to

break the circle is by making the roles themselves more enjoyable; then the need for a *quid pro quo* is bound to decrease.

(1975, 4)

Csíkszentmihályi's alternative to the reliance of extrinsic rewards and motivations was to study those who are highly motivated intrinsically, or who engage in autotelic activities. As he puts it, *Beyond Boredom and Anxiety* "began with the question: do activities for which extrinsic rewards are so minimal provide a set of intrinsic rewards of their own; if so, what are these intrinsic rewards?" (1975, 179). In pursuing this question, Csíkszentmihályi found a commonality between rock climbers, chess players, dancers, and surgeons; all of these activities allowed the individuals in question to enter a "flow" state. By flow, Csíkszentmihályi meant the experience of "a subjective state that people report when they are completely involved in something to the point of forgetting time, fatigue, and everything else but the activity itself" (Csíkszentmihályi, Abuhamdeh, and Nakamura 2014, 230). He described flow as involving a "merging of action and awareness" through which an individual "does not operate with a dualistic perspective: one is very aware of one's actions, but not of the awareness itself" (Csíkszentmihályi 2014, 138).[3] Looking at interview and questionnaire data, Csíkszentmihályi concluded that those who enter flow states:

> concentrate their attention on a limited stimulus field, forget personal problems, lose their sense of time and of themselves, feel competent and in control, and have a sense of harmony and union with their surroundings.
> (Csíkszentmihályi 1975, 182)

The kinds of activities that allow for "flow" are, according to Csíkszentmihályi, those that match the individual's skill level, allow for high levels of focus or a narrowing of attention, are goal based, and provide timely and clear feedback to the individual (1975, 182).

As Sam Binkley notes, flow has been praised by prominent public figures such as Tony Blair and Bill Gates, and several global firms—including "Toyota, Microsoft, Patagonia, and the Gallup Organization"—have praised flow for its capacity to promote "creativity and innovation among workers" (2014, 86). However, while many business leaders understand flow as a state to be induced within the workplace—thereby maintaining a distinction between work and leisure—Csíkszentmihályi argued for the broader restructuring of societies towards the production of flow and via the overcoming of the distinction between work and play (1975, 195). "Too often," writes Csíkszentmihályi, "it has been assumed that "mental health" or happiness means simply a passive adaptation to social demands, a normative adjustment to the status quo" (1975, 196). Missing from such approaches to "mental health" and happiness, on Csíkszentmihályi's account, is due consideration for the individual's capacity to feel a sense of agency and efficacy. As he writes, "perhaps the most salient element of the flow state is a sense of control over the environment. A person has to feel that his ability to act is adequate to meet the opportunities for action available" (1975, 191). Despite the need to ensure that environments are controllable, such that they better afford opportunities for flow, this emphasis on control does not suggest a self-reflective or analytic perspective for Csíkszentmihályi. Instead:

> the ability to control the environment—by limiting the stimulus field, finding clear goals and norms, and developing appropriate skills—is one side of the flow experience. The other side, paradoxically, is a feeling which seems to make the sense of control irrelevant. Many of the people we interviewed, especially those who most enjoy whatever they are doing, mentioned that at the height of their involvement with the activity they lose a sense of themselves as separate entities, and feel harmony and even a merging of identity with the environment.
>
> (1975, 194)

From Csíkszentmihályi's account, we can see the proximity between flow's purported capacity to mitigate anxiety and boredom—threats that Csíkszentmihályi locates within the very structure of late-capitalist societies—and the ethics of resonance, vulnerability, and entanglement discussed by Roquet, Hagood, Flore, and Rosa. Flow offers greater freedom through a strategy of becoming-ambient and becoming-environmental, insofar as the institution or firm is enjoined to produce environments that allow for maximum flow, and the individual is enjoined to embrace such environmental affordances to align their attention and action. In aligning attention and action, Csíkszentmihályi seems to imply that a range of modern dichotomies—such as freedom versus control, leisure versus work, and playfulness versus seriousness—can be overcome. For example, Csíkszentmihályi critiques Weber's analysis of the role of the "puritan work ethic" within capitalism (1975, 186). As Csíkszentmihályi recounts it, Weber's argument holds that the protestant reformation allowed for work, traditionally considered a "painful but necessary task," to be reimagined as "the main purpose of life" (1975, 186). Before the protestant reformation, work and salvation were viewed as two unrelated tasks. After the reformation, writes Csíkszentmihályi, "it became possible to redefine the two activities as mutually supportive: success in worldly affairs became a sign of election to eternal life" (1975, 186). For the modern capitalist worker, the centrality of work in life assured one not only of material comfort, but also of moral superiority—such that one could become both a slave to God and mammon.

The conventional account presents bourgeois culture and ideology as naturalising a life of constant work, prudence, and self-sacrifice—in other words, as governed by an ascetic ideal that suppresses enjoyment. However, for Csíkszentmihályi, such an understanding begins from, rather than analytically uncovers, a distinction between the ascetic ideal and enjoyment. As he writes, "Weber himself—probably because he also accepted the play-pleasure versus work-unpleasure dichotomy—never saw clearly that the ascetic withdrawal from all pleasure can in itself be enjoyable" (1975, 187). While an activity like academic research or painting may involve a great deal of hard work and self-discipline—and, to be pursued in earnest, may involve the relinquishing of pleasures like spending time with loved ones or relaxing at the beach, such that one's pursuit of their intellectual or artistic goals leads them to a somewhat monastic existence—Csíkszentmihályi maintains that, for the individual involved, "the serious work they do is more enjoyable for them than any form of leisure could be" (1975, 187). Medical work, legal work, and a whole range of vocations can be included in this analysis for Csíkszentmihályi. Indeed, the tragedy, as Csíkszentmihályi sees it, is that too few work environments and careers are designed in such a way as to facilitate this enjoyable ascetic existence.

To borrow the title of the concluding chapter of Csíkszentmihályi's *Beyond Boredom and Anxiety*, while Csíkszentmihályi wishes to develop a politics of enjoyment, such that we can more clearly see the stakes involved in overcoming the distinction between play and work, his text provides a somewhat simplistic and negative account of enjoyment as antithetical to anxiety, boredom, or pain. As such, while Csíkszentmihályi helps us to overcome a crude opposition between the renunciation of the ascetic and the experience of enjoyment, his work nevertheless maintains what appears to be a rigid distinction between enjoyment and pain. For this reason, we can provide a more nuanced account of such a politics by turning to another account of enjoyment and the ascetic ideal—from Csíkszentmihályi's understanding of Weber, to Alenka Zupančič's discussion of Friedrich Nietzsche and his critique of the ascetic ideal. Like Csíkszentmihályi, albeit to very different ends, Zupančič argues that, while the ascetic ideal might involve the curtailing of pleasure, this can conceal the possibility that, in foregoing fun in favour of a morning jog, maintaining one's sensible sleep routine, eating foods low in sugar, saturated fats, and caffeine, for example, the ascetic subject substitutes pleasure for enjoyment (2003, 47). Further developing one aspect of Freud's economic model of pleasure—as can be found in a text like "Beyond the Pleasure Principle," for example (Freud 2001)—which associates unpleasure with excitation and pleasure with the diminishment of excitation, Zupančič is interested in enjoyment as an affirmation of the excitations and tensions that are more commonly associated with pain (Zupančič 2003, 47). For Zupančič, if we are open to the possibility of such an inverted form of pleasure, then we can better grasp what is at stake in Nietzsche's account of the ascetic ideal. As she writes:

> if, according to Nietzsche, all great religions are an answer to man's feelings of displeasure and pain, they never treat the cause of this displeasure.

The Agonies of Freedom and Control 71

> Instead, they soothe the sensation of displeasure—they soothe it by providing an even stronger sensation. They literally '*outscream*' the displeasure (and the 'depression'—this is Nietzsche's term—linked to it) with an even sharper and more acute feeling, on account of which we no longer feel the previous displeasure. The religious (and especially Christian) cure for 'depressive discomfort' comes not in the form of an analgesic or a tranquiliser, but, rather, in the form of an 'irritating drug' or 'excitation-raiser', a stimulant. The ascetic ideal, writes Nietzsche, is *employed to produce orgies of feeling*.
>
> (Zupančič 2003, 47)

As opposed to eliminating pain, then, the ascetic ideal involves the adoption of practices that allow pain to be made meaningful—and, perhaps, even a source of duty or vocation—and to become affectively enticing. This is what Zupančič described as the "crucial aspect" of Nietzsche's account of the ascetic ideal: "not so much a negation of worldly life and its pleasures as their transformation into duty" (Zupančič 2003, 43). Here, Zupančič seems to be in agreeance with Csíkszentmihályi, insofar as the ascetic life of dedicated work can be more enjoyable than the pursuit of pleasurable leisure activities.

Zupančič's reading of Nietzsche is illuminating in the context of our previous discussion of ambient media, insofar as the ambient subject is able to access a range of technologies that facilitate the conversion of pain into forms of duty and competition. By quantifying one's daily steps, hours of sleep, minutes of mindfulness or meditation, the conversations one has had with loved ones and relatives—to provide just a few examples of the kinds of activities that ambient media can assist in tabulating and ranking—the individual is better able to externalise their duties to themselves, and to compete with themselves—thereby, in principle, achieving greater levels of wellbeing. However, and again like the feedback loops discussed in the previous chapter, Zupančič argues that the ascetic ideal often creates powerful compulsions that the individual becomes trapped within. As she puts it, in the ascetic ideal "discomfort is soothed (or silenced) by crises and states of emergency in which the subject feels *alive*. But this 'alive' is nothing other than 'undeadness,' the petrifying grip of surplus excitation and agitation" (Zupančič 2003, 49). We can better understand Zupančič when we reflect on the seemingly infinite capacity for self-help and wellness practices to produce new forms of discomfort that require further wellness interventions. New diets, exercise regimes, medications, and self-improvement activities all generate new forms of frustration, disappointment, and pain, and these forms of discomfort can easily facilitate the adoption of further tweaks to diet, medication, and routine. Indeed, with the aid of various forms of ambient media, the individual can also track the emergence of new disturbances, frustrations, and sites of intervention, by further quantifying, benchmarking, and self-competing in the pursuit of well-being solutions.

At first glance, it would seem that Zupančič and Csíkszentmihályi offer two contrasting accounts of the politics of enjoyment. Csíkszentmihályi's optimistic account appears to hold that a collective process of social planning could help unleash the powers of flow, thereby allowing for a more emotionally and ecologically sustainable world. Reading Csíkszentmihályi, one gets two very different images of the modern world. On the one hand, a world inhabited by a majority who do one thing—whether the "bullshit jobs" described by David Graeber (2018) that dominate the white collar world, or the low-wage and precarious drudgery that dominates the world of blue and pink collar work—and yet dream of doing something else; being an artist, perhaps, or pursuing a professional calling, in medicine or law, for instance. On the other hand, the world that Csíkszentmihályi wishes to make speculatively visible is one in which the spheres of education, work, and civil society have been designed such that individuals enter reciprocal relationships with their environments. On this account, the ascetic ideal can be reached other than through bribes and threats, and can instead be generalised through attention to the proper attunement of the individual to their task and the task to the environment.

However, Csíkszentmihályi appears to have developed concerns similar to those of Zupančič in works published after *Beyond Boredom and Anxiety*. In a 1985 article entitled, "Reflections on Enjoyment," Csíkszentmihályi raised the disquieting possibility that flow states could perhaps produce disastrous consequences. For instance, what if those designing systems for the production of mass death were primarily motivated by the flow states induced in attempting to solve incredibly difficult scientific and engineering problems? (1985, 489). Or what of soldiers in battle and criminals in peacetime who, according to Csíkszentmihályi, report enjoying the experiences of fighting or burglarising, insofar as "the clarity of life-and-death situations where each moment, each movement is meaningful and functional is a powerful stimulant" (1985, 489). While it would be "reassuring to condemn these as twisted, inhuman aberrations" or to relegate such enjoyment to the rank of an "instinctual heritage" and one that "we are shedding and shall eventually outgrow," Csíkszentmihályi insisted that we tarry with the possibility that the merging of attention and action and the attunement to one's environment experienced by a surgeon saving and patient's life and a burglar robbing the valuables of a sleeping family are both experiences of flow (1985, 490). In contrast to his more optimistic proclamations in *Beyond Boredom and Anxiety*, where he appeared to offer a call for the universalisation of flow, Csíkszentmihályi concludes "Reflections on Enjoyment" by commenting that while flow is a powerful means for achieving certain ends, it is by no measure "our most reliable guide" for assessing whether we should continue to pursue an activity (1985, 496). In this text, and like Zupančič, Csíkszentmihályi is concerned that flow states can lead to the limitless pursuit of further states of flow, such that, for Csíkszentmihályi, flow can become destructive and habit-forming:

this addictive property of the flow experience coupled with the unforeseen effects of technology result in an explosive combination. The solution of 'sweet problems' becomes an end in itself, regardless of consequences.

(1985, 495)

Flow, then, can both allow for a powerful and meaningful merging of the self with their environment, such that neither is reduced to a mere passive or inert object, with both interacting receptively and resonantly. Nevertheless, flow states can also foster relationships to the world that are painful, discomforting, or even violent and damaging, insofar as these latter experiences are rendered meaningful and enjoyable through the satisfaction of mastery and self-overcoming. As such, the question remains as to whether we can maintain a coherent sense of those forms of flow, or those kinds of ambient subjectivity, that are healthy, that lead to happiness, and that can interconnect to form an ecology of care, and those that can become themselves a form of alienation. While, at the level of consequences, we can of course maintain a distinction between heart surgery and robbery, or meditation and drug addiction, if flow or resonance is understood in an ethical register, then the question of separating flow from the "undeadness" described by Zupančič via Nietzsche becomes more challenging and urgent.

Flow on Effects

In this chapter, I have engaged with those accounts that view ambient media as having the potential to create, if not resonance, then at least a rekindled desire for resonant media environments. Surprisingly, perhaps, such an excursion has not resulted in a decision for or against ambient media as a means of emancipation, but had instead further complicated our understanding of the broader ecological or ambient turn within our understanding of and treatment of "mental illness." Indeed, while Rosa's work might seem opposed to that of Roquet, Hagood, Flore, or LaBelle—insofar as Rosa has little optimism for the political power of ambient media—both sets of discussions share a commitment to something like resonance as synonymous with the ethical and good life.

This is perhaps clearest in the work of Rosa, who provocatively begins *Resonance* by declaring that, with regards to late modernity, "if acceleration is the problem, resonance may well be the solution" (2019, 1). For Rosa, the absence of resonance, and the inability to find oneself resonating with the world and others, should be an issue of paramount importance for social theory. Rosa is so committed to this premise that he claims resonance is "always experienced as a fundamentally positive form of encountering the world," one that is opposed to alienation, which manifests as "indifference *or* repulsion" (2019, 447). Rosa is perhaps clearest in his commitment to this thesis when he discusses fascism in relation to the question of political resonance. Rosa acknowledges that many will view National Socialism as a disastrous project of political resonance. Against this view, Rosa insists that National Socialism was instead an example of the "pathology of resonance" (2019, 220). "From the very beginning," writes Rosa, "the Nazi movement was ideologically rooted not in resonance, but in *alienation*" (2019, 220). By "pathology of resonance" then, Rosa seems to mean a desire for resonance, rather than a form of resonance, that has become pathological, and manifests in the alienated experience of identitarian hatred.

Our earlier detour through the work of Csíkszentmihályi, Zupančič, and Nietzsche, has attempted to make clear why we should be suspicious of this bifurcation of alienation and resonance. As Simon Susen has argued—in a manner that echoes Csíkszentmihályi's concerns in "Reflections on Enjoyment":

> Rosa's assertion that it would be erroneous to assume that, in some cases, *experiences of violence* are tantamount to *experiences of resonance* is questionable. The point is not to deny the detrimental nature of violence, but to recognise that actors—on the giving or receiving end—may perceive its exercise as a source of resonance.
>
> (2020, 326)

The seemingly repressed ambivalences contained within resonance speaks to a potential flaw with much of the contemporary critical literature that discusses the intersection of contemporary alienation, "mental illness," and media. Insofar as it has become almost unthinkable within such literature to challenge a positive conception of weakness—one understood not only in terms of incapacity or fragility, but in terms of the responsiveness, receptivity, and openness we associate with care or empathy—the default progressive interrogation of "mental illness" appears to be one of asking whether the discourses and technologies of treatment *truly* facilitate healthy relationships. Regardless of whether or not one believes that ambient media produce such relationships in the present, the stakes of the critical discourse around "mental illness" presented by figures like Rosa, Roquet, Hagood, Flore, and LaBelle, presuppose the existence of clearly distinguishable open and bound, or emancipated and subjugated, modes of relationality. Whether we are discussing resonance versus alienation, or the strong versus weak self, the question remains on what terms can ambient media move us from one pole to another. For this reason, the possibility that relationality might be fundamentally ambivalent, or, indeed, that ambivalence might itself be constitutive of relationality, appears marginalised in their respective accounts.

Such a possibility would greatly destabilise the turn towards ambient conceptions of "mental illness" as environmental illness. If we take "mental illnesses" to be fundamentally relational—even taking into account an expanded notion of relationality that contends with a "general ecology" of human and non-human, and organic and inorganic existence—but we are unable to delineate an alienated from an unalienated mode of relationality, we are left with the question of how to properly assess the relative success and failure of mediated forms of therapy. If we view mute, hostile, repulsive, and painful experiences as inextricably connected to relationality—even those that appear to be resonant and privilege listening and responding, or those that promise the possibility of a "freedom beyond control"—then the question posed by ambient media is perhaps not, whether such media can facilitate resonance or a collective desire for resonance, but, instead, can ambient media produce resonance that is, perhaps paradoxically, also alienating and violent?

In response to this question, in the final chapter I will analyse a case study that connects this book's central themes: environmental illness and alienation, ambient media, the dominance of digital media in contemporary culture, and the ambivalence of resonance. Identified by the name QAnon, the last chapter will explore the cultural and political activities of an international group—albeit one primarily located in the USA—that arose in the wake of the election of Donald Trump as the 45th president of the United States. Labelled a cult, terrorist organisation, and augmented reality game, QAnon has attracted thousands of socially marginalised individuals into a digitally mediated political project and community. While its participants often speak of QAnon as imbuing their lives with a sense of transformative purpose that could be likened to resonance—and as pertaining to a collective project of transforming our media ecologies, in a manner comparable to Roquet's emancipatory description of ambient media—its practical consequences have often been alarming. Accordingly, in exploring QAnon, the last chapter will attempt to interrogate, not "mental illness" as environmental and relational, but relationality as itself always already open to, and as a precondition for, alienation.

Notes

1 For example, the ASMR account Sand Tagious' video "Very Satisfying and Relaxing Compilation 148 Kinetic Sand ASMR"—a video that comprises mostly of knives and other implements interacting with sand without a clear human presence—has 105 million views as of writing.
2 For example, consider: *Cannibal Capitalism: How Our System Is Devouring Democracy, Care, and the Planet—and What We Can Do About It* (Fraser 2022), *The Care Crisis: What Causes it and How Can We End it?* (Dowling 2022), *The Philosophy of Care* (Boys 2022), *Care and Capitalism* (Lynch 2021), and *The Psychopath Factory: How Capitalism Organizes Empathy* (Adams 2016) for just a handful of recent examples that think through the crisis of contemporary capitalism in terms of care and empathy.
3 Since I am drawing a connection between Rosa's resonance and the notion of flow, it is important to emphasise that flow does not involve a dissolution of the self into the activity or environment. If this were the case, flow should be seen as something

radically different to resonance, as the latter requires two voices that transform each other whilst maintaining their own efficacy. However, here we can see that flow requires the individual to maintain their awareness while engaging in a task or with their environment, but not in a self-conscious way. In other words, flow states seem to involve a heightened level of awareness, but one entwined with something other—and this is very different to the kind of self-awareness one might experience as they frustratingly wait for the workday to end.

References

Adams, Tristam. 2016. *The Psychopath Factory: How Capitalism Organises Empathy*. London: Repeater Books.
Berlant, Lauren. 2011. *Cruel Optimism*. Durham: Duke University Press.
Binkley, Sam. 2014. *Happiness as Enterprise: An Essay on Neoliberal Life*. Albany: State University of New York Press.
Brown, Wendy. 2015. *Undoing the Demos: Neoliberalism's Stealth Revolution*. New York: Zone Books.
Bull, Michael. 2013. "iPod Use: An Urban Aesthetics of Sonic Ubiquity". *Continuum* 27.4: 495–504.
Csíkszentmihályi, Mihály. 1975. *Beyond Boredom and Anxiety: The Experience of Play Work and Games*. San Fransisco: Jossey-Bass Publishers.
Csíkszentmihályi, Mihály. 1985. "Reflections on Enjoyment". *Perspectives in Biology and Medicine* 28.4: 489–497.
Csíkszentmihályi, Mihály, Abuhamdeh, Sami, Nakamura, Jeanne. 2014. "Flow". In *Flow and the Foundations of Positive Psychology: The Collected Works of Mihaly Csikszentmihalyi Perspectives in Biology and Medicine*. Ed. Mihály Csíkszentmihályi. New York: Springer. 227–238.
Dowling, Emma. 2022. *The Care Crisis: What Caused It and How Can We End It?* London: Verso.
Flore, Jacinthe. 2021. "Ingestible Sensors, Data, and Pharmaceuticals: Subjectivity in the Era of Digital Mental Health". *New Media & Society* 23.7: 2034–2051.
Fraser, Nancy. 2022. *Cannibal Capitalism: How Our System Is Devouring Democracy, Care, and the Planet - And What We Can Do About It*. London: Verso.
Freborg, Beverley. Et al. 2017. "An Examination of Personality Traits Associated with Autonomous Sensory Meridian Response (ASMR)". *Frontiers in Psychology* 8.247: 1–9.
Freud, Sigmund. 2001. *The Standard Edition of the Complete Works of Sigmund Freud Volume XII: Case History of Schreber, Papers on Technique and Other Works*. Trans. James Strachey. London: Vintage.
Graeber, David. 2018. *Bullshit Jobs: A Theory*. London: Penguin.
Groys, Boris. 2022. *The Philosophy of Care*. London: Verso.
Hagood, Mack. 2019. *Hush: Media and Sonic SelfControl*. Durham: Duke University Press.
LaBelle, Brandon. 2018. *Sonic Agency: Sound and Emergent Forms of Resistance*. London: Goldsmiths Press.
Lopez, German. 2018. "ASMR, Explained: Why Millions of People Are Watching YouTube Videos of Someone Whispering". *Vox*, 25 May. https://www.vox.com/2015/7/15/8965393/asmr-video-youtube-autonomous-sensory-meridian-response

Lynch, Kathleen. 2021. *Care and Capitalism*. London: Polity.
Manon, Hugh S. 2018. "ASMR Mania, Trigger-Chasing, and the Anxiety of Digital Repletion". In *Lacan and the Non-Human*. Eds. Gautam Basu Thakur and Jonathan Michael Dickstein. London: Palgrave. 227–248.
Roquet, Paul. 2016. *Ambient Media: Japanese Atmospheres of the Self*. Minneapolis: University of Minnesota Press.
Rosa, Hartmut. 2019. *Resonance: A Sociology of Our Relationship to the World*. Trans. James Wagner. Oxford: Polity Press.
Rosa, Hartmut. 2020a. *The Uncontrollability of the World*. Trans. James Wagner. Oxford: Polity Press.
Susen, Simon. 2020. "The Resonance of Resonance: Critical Theory as a Sociology of World-Relations?" *International Journal of Politics, Culture, and Society* 33: 309–344.
Weidenbaum, Marc. 2014. *Selected Ambient Works Volume II*. London: Bloomsbury.
Zappavigna, Michelle. 2020. "Digital Intimacy and Ambient Embodied Copresence in YouTube videos: Construing Visual and Aural Perspective in ASMR Role Play Videos". *Visual Communication* 22.2: 297–321.
Zupančič, Alenka. 2003. *The Shortest Shadow: Nietzsche's Philosophy of the Two*. Cambridge: MIT Press.

4 QAnon

From the Resonant to the Digitally Sublime

Influenced by Weber's *The Protestant Ethic and the "Spirit" of Capitalism* (2002) and Taylor's *Secular Age* (2007) Rosa's account of an accelerating but mute world maintains a narrative of disenchantment. "Weber's notion of disenchantment" Rosa writes, "bears all the hallmarks of a loss of resonance" and "expresses the changes in the *quality of our relationship to the world* which are inherently associated with this process. Disenchantment means that the world literally stops singing" (2019, 326). As has been discussed earlier in this book, if one of the important challenges raised by the notion of environmental illness is that of avoiding biological *and* sociological forms of reductionism, then it is incumbent on us to critically reflect on this notion of disenchantment. Indeed, early twenty-first century theoretical works in religious studies, such as Eugene McCarraher's *The Enchantments of Mammon: How Capitalism Became the Religion of Modernity* (2019); political theory, such as Jane Bennett's *The Enchantment of Modern Life: Attachments, Crossings, and Ethics* (2001); and anthropology,such as William Mazzarella's *The Mana of Mass Society* (2017) have attempted to do just this, proposing in heterogenous ways that a necessary link between modernisation and disenchantment is one of modernity's great myths. A clear forerunner to these critical accounts of disenchantment is of course Bruno Latour's *We Have Never Been Modern* (1993). For Latour, Westerners maintain an arrogant belief that they are truly different from non-Westerners and "premoderns" insofar as they, and only they, endure a truly disenchanted world (1993, 114). As Latour asked, "what psychologist will be subtle enough to explain our morose delight in being in perpetual crisis and in putting an end to history?" (1993, 114).

Such a question should not be read as an attempt to disregard the disenchanting forces of modernity. Perhaps disenchantment has always existed, such that modernity merely has its own technologies of disenchantment rather than a monopoly on disenchantment as such. Or, perhaps, disenchantment is unique to modernity, and pre-modern forms of ratiocination, organisation, and demythologisation have to be understood as qualitatively different to the processes of disenchantment. Bracketing these possibilities for the moment, it is useful to take seriously the notion that, within modernity and postmodernity, disenchantment has never been totalising. If we do take seriously disenchantment as simply one possibility within modern and postmodern culture—and, to follow Latour's point, perhaps even a possibility that can become a source of enchantment, albeit a sadomasochistic one—we can better question the hope a figure like Rosa has for resonance. As such, in this chapter we will look to QAnon to reconsider these oppositions between disenchantment and enchantment, alienated and resonant relationships, and notions of pathological and healthy relationality. QAnon is useful as a focal point to assist us in investigating these oppositions for a range of reasons. Firstly, its participants routinely discuss their entrance into this online culture as something like a transition from a mute relationship with a hostile world to a resonant relationship with a world that is open and transformative. Secondly, QAnon has emerged primarily through ambient media by way of smartphones, dashcams, and social media platforms, all of which have vastly increased our capacity to connect events and information that are otherwise politically, geographically, and historically disparate. Lastly, QAnon appears especially appropriate as a focus for our inquiries given the well-documented "mental health" challenges experienced by many of its adherents, and due to it attracting a seemingly disproportionate number of well-being and lifestyle "experts" into its orbit. As such, QAnon has always been connected to contemporary experiences of alienation, and the attempt to find new mediated responses to the experience of "mental illness."

What Is QAnon?

QAnon can be understood as an online conspiracy theory—that is, as a particular narrative about world events and the powerful people orchestrating them—and as a network of adherents who have produced a shared culture of engaging with QAnon lore. While QAnon's popularity is mostly limited to the United States, the journalist Will Sommer reports that online culture has adherents in Australia, Canada, Great Britain, Brazil, Germany, Finland, and Japan (2023, 197–199).[1] Emerging in 2017 on the imageboard 4chan, QAnon started as a series of anonymous posts by a figure initially using the moniker Q Clearance Patriot, shortened later simply to Q. As Mike Wendling reports for the *BBC*, the anonymous 4chan user Q "claimed to have a level of US security approval known as 'Q clearance'. These messages became known as 'Q drops' or 'breadcrumbs', often written in cryptic language peppered with slogans, pledges and pro-Trump themes" (Wendling 2021). Q's first post predicted the arrest of Hilary Clinton, and as the QAnon conspiracy grew it would come to connect an expansive array of political elites and celebrities (Bloom and Moskalenko 2021, 2). As Nicholas Smith has summarised, QAnon's central beliefs are that: (1) Hilary Clinton and other elite figures in American public life engage in child trafficking and ritual sacrifice in order to extract adrenochrome—which, according to QAnon lore, provides the user with eternal youth, a powerful high, or even a cure for COVID-19 (Bloom and

Moskalenko 2021, 30); (2) these public figures were to be arrested and brought to justice by Donald J. Trump during an event referred to as *the storm*—and that was widely believed to occur sometime before or during the 2020 US presidential election; (3) COVID-19 is fake, or, if it is real, the COVID-19 pandemic was orchestrated (Smith 2022, 361). While these central beliefs seem to be shared by the vast majority of QAnon adherents, QAnon is in many ways a pastiche of existing conspiracy theories, incorporating, amongst other things, David Icke's ideas around a secret race of reptilians who control the world (Icke 2014) and JFK assassination theories—including the notion that JFK Jr never died and faked his own death in order to "avenge his father's assassination by the deep state" (Sommer 2023, 47).

As we will go on to discuss later in this chapter, a key component of QAnon's appeal has been its capacity to accommodate a wide range of popular conspiracy theories and culture war tropes. Due both to the cryptic nature of Q's online messages and to the participatory logics underpinning the ambient media used to share and interpret these Q drops, QAnon lore has proven flexible and capable of accommodating an expansive array of ideas. In this way, QAnon favours ambient attention and ambient intimacy, insofar as a broad, but perhaps shallow, understanding of history, politics, natural science—especially biology—and popular culture assists the individual QAnon adherent to engage with the emerging crowd-sourced lore. Similarly, QAnon offers connection and intimacy to its adherents, albeit in distributed or spatiotemporally distanced way. To retrieve a canonical distinction from media theory, Q drops and crowd-sourced QAnon messages—as with the likes, shares, and views that hierarchise them—can be understood as cool media (McLuhan 1994, 22–23). Unlike hot media, which McLuhan defined as high definition and low in participation—insofar as the relative completeness of the message in question inhibits the viewer's need to fill in what is missing—cool media encourage participation due to a relatively lower level of definition, hence a greater openness for the viewer or audience to project or insert their own meaning (McLuhan 1994, 22–23).[2] Such coolness helps to facilitate "produsage," which, for the cultural theorist Joseph Vogl—influenced by Axel Bruns who coined the portmanteau of production and usage (2008)—is one of the underpinnings logics of the digital platform economy. As Vogl writes:

> unlike industrial production, these activities for producing digital content [...] are characterised by ubiquitous access and low thresholds for entry, by being informal, occasional, and without temporal or spatial constraints, and by their reference to anything that can be performed online.
>
> (2022, 54)

As such, and putting aside whether one finds conspiracy theories to be unconvincing in general, the "low threshold to entry" mentioned by Vogl exists both at the level of the ambient character of the media in question—the ubiquity of smartphones, and the relative ease of sharing information via social media and streaming platforms, for example—and at the epistemological level. Indeed, QAnon does not offer a clear-cut narrative, but instead connects a growing range of concerns to a revolving cast and some central themes. Moreover, QAnon appears to allow the individual to both "fill in the gaps" within QAnon lore—insofar as Q drops and the broader lore itself are incomplete, low-definition, or cool in McLuhan's terms—and to "fill in the gaps" in their own lives, that is to say, to provide resonance where only mute relationships existed. In this way, the conspiracy theory and its accompanying culture has provided meaning and purpose for a base of followers who seem to overtly understand themselves to be alienated—that is, living in a society that is fundamentally out of joint, and in which it is difficult to maintain reciprocal and transformative relationships with others (Bloom and Moskalenko 2021, 17, 42). As Bloom and Moskalenko argue, many QAnon followers express feelings of disconnection from broader society and an underlying sense that the world is inhospitable. Through a range of case studies, Bloom and Moskalenko depict QAnon participants as suffering disproportionately from "psychological disorders" such as "Munchausen by proxy, substance abuse, depression, anxiety, PTSD, and bipolar disorder" (2021, 137). Furthermore, and drawing on a report by National Consortium for the Study of Terrorism and Responses to Terrorism (START) Bloom and Moskalenko claim that the majority of QAnon adherents who participated in the 2020 January 6 attack on the US State Capitol building had prior "mental illness" diagnoses (2021, 137). As the START report "QAnon Offenders in the United States" explains, "nearly two-thirds of the 44 QAnon offenders who committed crimes before and after the Capitol insurrection have documented "mental health" concerns" (Jensen and Kane 2021, 3).

QAnon has not simply attracted participants who disproportionately, if not exclusively, experience the world as alienating and hostile. QAnon offers further the majority of its participants with a sense of empowerment and belonging, and this has been made possible primarily due to the conspiracy theory's connection to online wellness culture. As several commentators have indicated, QAnon lore is incredibly popular among yoga, alternative medicine, and self-help social media influencers (Dickinson 2021; Meltzer 2021; Wiseman 2021). While the typically angry paranoia of QAnon might appear to have little in common with the more peaceful and hopeful outlook of new age, alternative medicine, and wellness culture, Charlotte Ward's and David Vaos' notion of "conspirituality" may help us to better understand the connection. For Ward and Vaos, while conspiracy theory and new age spirituality—especially the various forms of holistic belief and practice that holds the body, mind, and universe to be one—share the assumptions that "nothing happens by accident, nothing is as it seems, and everything is connected," the entanglement of conspiracy theory and spirituality has perhaps emerged due to the capacity for the former's "political cynicism" to be "tempered" by the latter's "spiritual optimism" (2011, 108). For Ward and Vaos, the conspiracy theorist and author David Icke gave expression to this confluence of political cynicism and spiritual optimism in the 1990s, reflecting that:

> when I meet people who are investigating the conspiracy but are not into the spiritual, I find people full of paranoia, full of fear ... because they can't see the spiritual solutions ... When I meet so many people in the New Age area ... I often find people who, so often, think that if you address the negative, then that's really bad. You must only address the positive ... But if you don't address the negative, either the negative gets more negative or stays as it is. What you don't do is change it.
>
> (Quoted in Ward and Vaos 2011, 108)

Accordingly, rather than viewing the world as a dark and inhospitable place, as might be the case with many conspiracy theorists, or of disconnecting from the world by focusing on the self-as-world—in as much as new age holism views the self and its desires as inherently connected to something cosmological and eternal—conspirituality movements like QAnon provide a means for the alienated individual to connect, and perhaps resonate, with a world that is rife with injustice and discord. Following Icke, it would seem that an interest in conspiracy theory alone can empower the individual—who, at the very least, feels they can understand the true nature of reality—but leaves them without a sense that the world is truly transformable and open. An exclusive interest in new age spirituality, by contrast, reveals the world as open and dynamic, but can reduce the individual to simply accommodating a cosmic will. Arguably, conspirituality brings these two modes of comportment together, such that the individual and the world each has a voice that could be allowed or enabled to resonate. For example, the former Wall Street banker and Citibank employee Jason Gelinas is quoted by Bloom and Moskalenko as saying that:

> like many of you, I felt that something wasn't right in the world, that our country was headed in the wrong direction [...] then something magical happened in 2016 that defied expectations—a complete outsider to the political establishment, Donald J. Trump, won the presidential election! Amazing. A glimmer of light in the darkness.
>
> (Quoted in Bloom and Moskalenko 2021, 17)

Gelinas' reference to the figure of light expresses a key connection between QAnon and conspirituality, which, as Paolo Demuru points out, is ubiquitous in a range of alternative therapy and new age communities (2022, 597–598). As Demuru writes, "wellness and alt. health influencers who embraced QAnon and other conspiratorial narratives during the COVID-19 pandemic stopped using the term 'light' to refer only to spiritual awakening, giving it a distinctly political tone" (2022, 597). As previously mentioned, QAnon adherents like Gelinas view their connection to the lore as inspiring a more open and transformative relationship to the world, and, importantly, one through which alienation can be understood and overcome politically, and not just through a spiritual accommodation of the status quo.

As we will discuss later in the chapter, QAnon cannot be separated from violence and paranoia, with the latter culminating in the events of January 6. Nevertheless, QAnon has given its adherents a sense of self-efficacy, purpose, and connection. As Bloom and Moskalenko have argued, QAnon provides its participants with *cognitive utility*, in that it allows them to feel like our increasingly complex and overwhelming world is understandable, *social utility*, insofar as forms of community and connection in neoliberal societies are increasingly troubled by isolation and loneliness—painful experiences that were only intensified throughout the COVID-19 lockdowns—*emotional utility*, by way of promising a utopian end to the pain and suffering of the world, and *personal utility* in that QAnon provided a narrative of redemption for the enormous number of its adherents who suffer with addiction issues, diagnosed "mental illnesses," and personal tragedy (2021, 106–112). All of which raises the question of how to situate QAnon with regards to environmental illness and alienation as articulated by a figure like Rosa. Given that vast numbers of people have turned to ambient media in order to overcome loneliness and despair, to collectively shape their lives, and to produce new atmospheres of thought and feeling that allow the self and world to appear intertwined in a process of mutual transformation, can we view QAnon as revealing a supressed ambivalence within Rosa's theory of resonance? Or, drawing on Rosa, should we understand QAnon as an extreme symptom of ambient media's capacity to produce echo-chambers of pseudo-resonance?

Atmospheres of Information

David Fincher's 1997 film *The Game* centres on a wealthy investment banker's struggles to escape a web of fiction, conspiracy, and blackmail. The film's protagonist, Nicholas Van Orton, is gifted a voucher for the services of Consumer Recreation Services (CRS) by his ne'er-do-well brother Conrad. On meeting Jim Feingold, CRS's vice-president of engineering and data analysis, Van Orton is informed that CRS provides its customers with a game, a kind of alternate reality vacation that changes with each user and provides "whatever's lacking" (1997). Although Van Orton is initially rejected as a CRS customer—supposedly due to failing to pass the company's standard physical and psychological safety tests—Van Orton finds himself embroiled in a terrifying series of events, all of which pose the question of whether CRS is providing him with an exciting experience akin to real life video game, or whether CRS is a con, an elaborate scam that extracts millions from wealthy individuals foolish enough to find themselves targeted, and desperate to pay any amount of money to make the "game" end. While *The Game* was limited to cult classic status in the 1990s—overshadowed by Fincher's films *Se7en* (1995) and *Fight Club* (1999)—it has only appeared more prophetic in the years following the election of Donald J. Trump. Like *The Game*, QAnon's origins have been linked both to a kind of alternate reality game (ARG) and to a scam intended to manipulate the naïve and vulnerable for political purposes and monetary gain. As the game designer Reed Berkowitz notes for *The Washington Post*, QAnon, like ARG used for marketing purposes, encourage individuals to look for clues and puzzles in the real world (2021). Once the players are engaged, Berkowitz observes, it is difficult to direct their attention away from random patterns and towards the puzzles and clues purposefully planted (2021). Like Van Orton in *The Game*, QAnon's adherents appear to struggle to separate coincidence from conspiracy—especially since QAnon blurs seemingly baseless ideas about elite figures with established facts, such as the crimes committed by Jeffrey Epstein. For ARG players and QAnon adherents, Berkowitz reflects, the empowerment to participate in the construction of meaning, and the expansiveness of the gaming environment, means the boundaries of alternate reality and reality become difficult to maintain; often, the players "hadn't seen a clue—they'd created one in their minds. They hadn't followed the plot of the story or solved a puzzle; they'd created chaos. But it felt the same to them" (Berkowitz 2021).

While it is important to avoid a technologically deterministic understanding of QAnon, I would argue that what I have called the ambient media condition has played a major role—alongside cultural, economic, and epistemological shifts that I will discuss later in this chapter—in transforming today's dominant modes of sociality. As Hugh Davies puts it:

> the emergence of ARGs at the turn of the millennium occurred against a backdrop of paradigm shifts in the entertainment industry that saw prosumers, hackers, modders and DIY content makers, become central to the nature of networked information and entertainment. Once a fringe phenomenon, QAnon signals the mainstreaming of the ARG form.
>
> (Davies 2022, 74)

Put differently, while QAnon has clear game design elements—privileging puzzles and cryptograms in the dissemination of its lore, for instance—it is important to situate QAnon within a broader media context, one in which, through ambient media, game logics appear to underpin an expanding number of social phenomena. One of the most insightful, albeit bizarre, analyses of QAnon's relationship to this broader gaming culture has come from Wu Ming, a small offshoot of the anonymous artist and activist collective Luther Blisset. Luther Blisset was a collective artistic project mostly based in Italy in the 1990s and that involved, among other things, elaborate pranks and hoaxes that would lure credulous and profit-driven media companies to disseminate falsehoods. In what could be their most elaborate project, 1997 saw the Luther Blisset collective organise a fake satanic panic in the town of Viterbo near Rome by orchestrating both a series of "black masses" and a fake catholic advocacy group called the "Committee for the Sanctity of Morals" that documented devil worship and alerted the media. As Eddy Frankel writes for *The Art Newspaper*, "a film of one of the black masses even made its way onto primetime Italian television news programmes. But it was all fake: the Satanists and the vigilantes alike" (2021). According to one of the members of the Blisset offshoot Wu Ming, referred to as Wu Ming 1, the goal of such interventions was to instil a critical distance from certain cultural fixations—like satanic panics—but to do so, not by fact checking, promoting media literacy, or educating the public in a conventional sense, but by creating "very complex, even cumbersome life-sized practical jokes to create a kind of chain reaction of falsehoods. We called these *ambienti*, or informational environments, in order to inhabit them and live in them for long periods" (Quoted in Haiven et al. 2022, 258). There is of course a clear proximity between the curation of such informational surrounds, environments, or *ambienti* and the worldbuilding of QAnon. However, a far stranger connection between the two projects exists in the form of Blisset's anonymously coauthored 1999 novel *Q*, a text set during the reformation and that depicts a Catholic "*agent-provocateur*" who infiltrates a radical movement, all the while sending communications back to the Vatican signed only with the letter Q (Haiven et al. 2022, 257). The protagonist convinces the radicals to stage a violent conflict with their local "bishops and corrupt authorities" but the uprising is a trap (Haiven et al. 2022, 257). As Wu Ming 1 observes, this is:

> *exactly* the premise of QAnon's narrative: An anonymous figure, sending dispatches signed "Q," posing as a guy who has access to very valuable confidential information from the very top level of state power. But, in fact, he spreads disinformation. As in our collectively written novel, he tricks his targets into taking the field for an ultimate battle: 6 January 2021 on Capitol Hill.
> (Quoted in Haiven et al. 2022, 257).

Such eerie similarities at the level of form and content have raised questions around whether QAnon is a Luther Blisset-inspired project, or whether it may have been conceived by members of the Blisset collective—even if ultimately going rogue and escaping the collective's control. Regardless, Wu Ming 1's analysis is insightful, and it is worthwhile understanding their sympathy for QAnon, especially as relates to the question of enchantment. In a manner not unlike Roquet's aforementioned promotion of ambient media as a means of raising the problem of collective and emancipatory affective design, Wu Ming 1 approaches QAnon as an attempt to enchant the world, to "offer new angles from which to look at the world and the means to *feel* differently about reality" and in a way that is exciting, insofar as these collective fantasies "don't just answer the anger and frustration people feel with the world as it is (exploitation, discrimination, disenfranchisement, poverty, etc); they also answer the need for wonder, for magic, for enchantment" (Quoted in Haiven et al. 2022, 264). Against "ratiosuprematism" or the "belief in the supremacy of rationality at all times, no matter the issue and context" Wu Ming 1 espouses the need for anti-capitalist social movements connected to critical forms of enchantment that avoid merely channelling an "energy for real change" towards "false narratives based on scapegoating" (Quoted in Haiven et al. 2022, 262). Although Wu Ming 1 does not provide a direct comparison between QAnon and their own information *ambienti*, we can underline the significance of the Kantian dynamical sublime in Wu Ming 1's analysis to assist us in conceptualising critical and uncritical forms of enchanting information environments.

On Wu Ming 1's account, the dynamical sublime "names a pleasure that has an indirect origin, an indirect cause, because it arises from the feeling of (to paraphrase) a momentary arrest of vital energies, followed by a more intense exaltation" (Quoted in Haiven et al. 2022, 264). To illustrate this reading of the *Critique of Judgement*, Wu Ming 1 refers to Kant's example of watching a lightning storm from a safe vantage point. Through such an encounter, the individual in question experiences the affective intensity of nature's vastness and power, but from a shielded position of pleasurable contemplation. According to Wu Ming 1, if we substitute the power of the sphere of nature for the power of the sphere of politics, "you have QAnon's narrative" (Quoted in Haiven et al. 2022, 264). Drawing on the work of Daniël de Zeeuw and Alex Gekker, I would argue that what Wu Ming 1 associates with QAnon can be understood as a broader effect of ambient media, the experience of the "digital sublime," an encounter with the "endless maze of information" provided by the internet as "the vast and ever retreating horizon of the next hyperlink before the last" and through which one is beset by "a kind of epistemic vertigo that straddles the line between pleasure and paranoia" (Zeeuw and Gekker 2023, 7). As such, the experience of the digital sublime provides the awe and terror of seeing how things are connected, of who's behind it all, of how things really work.

In the final scenes of *The Game*, atop a skyscraper a pistol wielding Nicholas Van Orton prepares for what he takes as a final showdown between himself and CRS, or whoever the people tormenting and extorting him really are. At this point in the film, Van Orton has been convinced by a series of violent and disturbing events that CRS is a malevolent force that must be stopped, or, at the very least, confronted in an act of revenge. Despite being reassured that he is still in a game, Van Orton fires at what he takes to be an oncoming attacker only to realise that he has accidentally killed his brother

Conrad, who crashes to the ground in a white tuxedo with a celebratory bottle of champagne. Horrified, the CRS employees lament what went wrong and how Van Orton was able to outmanoeuvre the game's confines, and traumatised at the death of his brother, Van Orton attempts to commit suicide by jumping off the skyscraper and crashing through the glass ceiling of a ballroom situated beneath. Awakening in a giant cushion placed to soften his fall, Van Orton is greeted by Conrad and a host of well-wishers who congratulate him on finally completing the game. Even Conrad's apparent murder at the hands of his brother, and Van Orton's suicide attempt, were all meticulously planned plot points in the game's narrative. Van Orton seems to be transformed by the experience of playing the game, and even the act of attempting suicide—a re-enactment of his father's suicide, a tragedy referenced throughout the film—seems to have instilled in Van Orton a sense of closure regarding past pain and failure, and a more open and meaningful relationship with the world and others. Like *The Game*, QAnon seems to provide its participants with a resonance lacking in life, a sense that the world is open and transformable, that things are not as humdrum and disappointing as they may seem but dynamic and exciting, and that one can transform themselves just as QAnon transforms the world into a space replete with plots, secret organisations, and supernatural power. Unlike *The Game*, however, when QAnon adherents have come to understand themselves as part of a participatory fantasy, the violence is often all too real. For example, in what is arguably the urform of QAnon violence, Edgar Maddison Welch, who stormed Comet Ping Pong in 2016 in order to "rescue the children being abused in the pizzeria's basement," had to acknowledge that he had made a fundamental error when, after expelling several rifle rounds and terrifying customers, he realised that the pizzeria didn't have a basement (Sommer 2023, 9).[3] As Sommer notes, Welch later admitted that his "intel on this wasn't 100%" (Sommer 2023, 9). Given the physical violence and emotional pain caused to families, friends, and even strangers as a result of QAnon and related conspiracy theories, the enchanting aspects discussed by Wu Ming 1 have been understandably downplayed in favour of emphasising the threat that excessive volumes of information poses civil society and democracy. As such, the common refrain from academics and pundits has been for the need to increase media literacy, to defend reason and truth against misinformation and fantasy, and to promote a new ethical comportment that can respond adequately to the impacts of what I have been calling ambient media. Interestingly, there has been little call for resonance as a means of diverting QAnon adherents away from co-production of and active engagement with QAnon lore. Instead, and given that QAnon does seem to offer its adherents an experience of resonance, it is perhaps unsurprising that many academics and commentators have begun calling out for a kind of rational self-examination that resembles the mute detachment that Rosa associates with the modern alienated relationship to the world.

An Interesting Ethical Imperative

Published in 2021 as the COVID-19 pandemic was still considered a global health emergency, *When Bad Thinking Happens to Good People* is a philosophical investigation into what Steven Nadler and Lawrence Shapiro characterise as a contemporary "epistemological crisis" embodied in conspiratorial thinking such as that of QAnon's adherents (2021, 1). While delegating to others the burden of attempting to understand why so many fall into "bad thinking"—"has natural selection shaped us in ways that make poor reasoning as irresistible as the sweet and fatty foods responsible for escalating rates of diabetes, obesity, and other afflictions? These are questions for psychologists to answer" (2021, 204)—Nadler and Shapiro nevertheless espouse a need for a renewal of rationality, one grounded in self-knowledge and "knowing and following the canonical standards of rationality that lead to the responsible formation and defence of beliefs" (2021, 5–6). Rationality must be defended, they argue, since part of our contemporary predicament regarding fake news, post-truth, and conspiracy theory results from the fact that "a person's assessment of evidence [...] is often grounded not in epistemic factors but moral, ethical, political, and economic ones" (2021, 204).

Unaccompanied by a renewal of metaphysics, and by a new regime of censorship that would limit the number of statements competing for the status of evidence and truth, it is difficult to know exactly what a renewal of reason would look like. While Nadler and Shapiro promote "avoiding precipitous convictions [...] abandoning beliefs for which there is no evidence [...] developing the practice of good, logically sound reasoning," and so forth, the question of which philosophical position on evidence, logic, and truth can be trusted is never resolved (2021, 200). However, rather than viewing this as a fault of Nadler's and Shapiro's book, I would argue their lack of a fully developed metaphysics reveals, despite their own declarations, the ethical core of their project. Going further, I would argue that their work unconsciously embodies an ethical commitment that has arisen in response to ambient media and the concomitant saturation of information in contemporary liberal-capitalist societies. Indeed, while espousing the rational examination of one's self and world, Nadler and Shapiro acknowledge that "engaging in an examined life does not ask you (or forbid you) to do anything at all—other than engage in examination, of course" (2021, 172–173). As such, I would argue that their broader project promotes a minimal ethical project, one that centres on the need to engage in rational examination, but without commitments other than to the ethical value of examination itself. Far from being a commitment held only by philosophers, we can see that an ethics of examination without commitments—other than to examination, and certainty *not* to any strong metaphysical notion of truth—has become one of contemporary culture's dominant alternatives to the experience of the digital sublime offered by phenomena like QAnon.

Accordingly, and in order to contextualise this ethical response to fake news, post-truth, and conspiracy theory, it is useful to return to our discussion of ambient attention in Chapter 1, and the interconnected epistemological and affective demands that issue from the becoming-environmental of digital technology and information, on the one hand, and what I am calling a minimal ethics of examination without commitments, on the other. As argued in earlier chapters, the sheer volume of information one produces and encounters through ambient media—and the neoliberal ethics of self-responsibility that accompanies such access to information—has burdened individuals and groups with the injunction to affirm both novelty and truth. From one perspective, contemporary liberal societies construct an idealisation of the ethically informed consumer, who keeps themselves abreast of the latest news and trends by carefully monitoring social media, legacy news media, policy updates—encountered either in one's workplace or in the broader community—and one's own biometric data. From another perspective, the corrosive relativism of market logics has greatly contributed to an ethics of self-responsibility that sees individuals and institutions increasingly wary of conspiracy theory, fake news, and misinformation. With a weakened, if not absent, social safety net, the individual must carefully calibrate their investments and movements to ensure maximum return. In recent years, the rise of short-form video platforms like TikTok have created new cultural outlets for such an ethics of informational self-responsibility. Thousands of accounts amassing billions of views relay to the viewer the necessity of investing, managing one's finances, maintaining "healthy" diets and routines, and, most importantly, liking and subscribing to continually receive important tips, tricks, and life-hacks.

While ancient and enlightenment thinkers alike extolled the virtues of pursuing wisdom and truth over mere opinion or *doxa*, for the philosopher and media theorist Joseph Vogl, the economic requirements of an increasingly financialised society create the almost unavoidable burden of tarrying with gossip, opinion, and rumour (2022, 36). As Vogl argues, it has been understood since at least the writings of the seventeenth-century moral philosopher Joseph de la Vega that financial markets encourage the trader to familiarise themselves with all possible traditions and systems of knowledge, insofar as one should be capable of recourse to "politics, geography, nautical science, arithmetic, rhetoric, and jurisprudence" as required (2022, 33). Nevertheless, the epistemological and temporal logics of financial markets require that such scientific endeavours be placed alongside opinion and rumour. As Vogl writes, again with reference to de la Vega:

> the substance of stock-market information is thus constituted in the form of a "stock-market opinion" or "stock-market atmosphere," which, in the course of speculative dealings, in the "foaming waves of speculation," cannot distinguish the factual content of news from the event of its disclosure.
> (2022, 33)

Accordingly, alongside the logic of "dedifferentiation" identified by Fredric Jameson—through which the cultural, economic, and technological spheres become increasingly blurred—even minimal distinctions between reality and representation become unstable due to the market's performative logic (Jameson 2009, 86–87). As such, the all-encompassing and complex character of such atmospheres of information threaten focused attention in the form of expert knowledge and respect for disciplinary boundaries. While it is true that one must be able to reason, to take account of facts and to apply logical rules, Vogl points out that falsehoods or half-truths can be just as important, if not more so, in a financial market (2022, 33–34). Indeed, as the sociologist Will Davies has pointed out, financial speculators and entrepreneurs like Peter Thiel place great emphasis on those beliefs that go against consensus truth, insofar as the possibility of their becoming true in the market—even if only temporarily—heralds significant commercial advantages and profits (2018, 149–150). Accordingly, the subject of ambient media—embodied in *The Game*'s Nicholas Van Orton, an investment banker who profits from the becoming-ambient of information only to find himself imperilled by the vaporous intermixing of truth, fact, and fiction—encounters a tension between an ethical imperative and an epistemological problem. On the one hand, the injunction to stay informed—to maintain an ongoing process of having one's behaviour formed by an ever-changing and ever-expanding stock of information—and, on the other hand, the difficulty of distinguishing truth from falsehood *and* the difficulty of knowing whether acting upon a truth or a falsehood will be more beneficial in the short term. For Vogl then, it makes more sense to frame "economic judgement" in aesthetic rather than cognitive terms (Vogl 2022, 35). As he writes:

> put in Kantian terms, the form taken by this economic judgement therefore has little in common with cognitive judgments. If anything, it displays an aesthetic character, since judgments of taste (according to Kant) stake a claim to "general validity" by invoking an "indeterminate norm" that, itself conceptually indeterminate, could "demand universal assent."
>
> (Vogl 2022, 35)

Vogl clarifies his brief reference to Kant's third critique by way of John Maynard Keynes, and it is worth expounding on Keynes' theory of financial speculation from the *General Theory* to better understand Vogl's claim about market judgements as aesthetic. In chapter twelve of the *General Theory*, entitled "The State of Long-Term Expectation," Keynes notes that, given the difficulty encountered by anyone looking to make secure and profitable long-term investments, the investor typically concerns themselves "not with what an investment is really worth to a man who buys it 'for keeps', but with what the market will value it at, under the influence of mass psychology, three months or a year hence" (Keynes 1993, 154–155). For this reason, the investor must base their decisions on information that is more diffuse and amorphous than the expert or specialist may prefer. As Keynes writes, "the professional investor is forced to concern himself with the anticipation of impending changes, in the news or in the atmosphere, of the kind by which experience shows that the mass psychology of the market is most influenced" (Keynes 1993, 155). Foreshadowing Vogl's theory of financial epistemology, Keynes' here seems to be concerned with something similar to what we have been calling ambient attention. The capacity to distribute one's attention across multiple competing concerns, and without overemphasising any one of them, appears—like Benjamin's observations on cinema and Freud's observations on free association—in stock market trading as an example of the becoming ambient of attention as a broad cultural phenomenon. This capacity to spread out one's attention, to look sideways, as it were, is most clearly expressed by Keynes via his example of newspaper beauty competitions. As Keynes describes it, the kind of competition he has in mind runs as follows:

> the competitors have to pick out the six prettiest faces from a hundred photographs, the prize being awarded to the competitor whose choice most nearly corresponds to the average preferences of the competitors as a whole; so that each competitor has to pick, not those faces which he himself finds prettiest, but those which he thinks likeliest to catch the fancy of the other competitors, all of whom are looking at the problem from the same point of view. It is not a case of choosing those which, to the best of one's judgment, are really the prettiest, nor even those which average opinion genuinely thinks the prettiest. We have reached the third degree where we devote our intelligences to anticipating what average opinion expects the average opinion to be.
> (Keynes 1993, 156)

It is here that we can better understand in what way Vogl compares market judgements to Kantian aesthetic judgements. As Kant declares in *The Critique of Judgement*:

> whenever we make a judgement declaring something to be beautiful, we permit no one to hold a different opinion, even though we base our judgement only on our feeling rather than on concepts; hence we regard this underlying feeling as a common rather than as a private feeling.
> (1987, §22; 89)

Aesthetic judgements, for Kant, are born both of our subjective feeling—rather than the existence of concepts, as with a cognitive judgement—but also require something like social recognition. As Kant acknowledges, just because I feel something to be beautiful doesn't mean that others will agree, but they "*ought* to" (1987, §22; 89). Accordingly, aesthetic judgements reveal an important and productive tension between subjective feeling and social agreement insofar as aesthetic judgements are freed from the rules of cognitive judgements, but also require some kind of assent through the recognition of shared feeling. As Sophia Rosenfield writes in her political history of the notion of common sense, Kant's theory of aesthetic judgement suggests "the possibility of agreement founded on affective identification with the other, or intersubjectivity. It is a distinct way of knowing that has no rational ground" (2011, 223–224).

While the ideal of such intersubjective knowing might be a public sphere of free and open debate, following Vogl we can argue that interconnected rise of a dominant financial capitalism, and the atmospheres of information facilitated by ambient media, has privileged such aesthetic judgements, albeit along the lines of Keynes' newspaper competition. Whether or not information pertains to some truth is less relevant than whether it connects a multiplicity of judgements together such that—temporarily at least—something can be viewed as valuable. As Vogl writes about financial markets—although we can argue that the same is true for ambient media and their atmospheric production and circulation of information—"insofar as financial markets operate as systems for the production of financing prices, they may be understood as mechanisms for the autopoietic production of *doxa*, in which rational expectations and preferences are only truly rational if they directly coincide with common opinion and find consensus in normative ideas" (Vogl 2022, 35–36).[4] As with the example of Thiel, market judgements require both the subjective feeling that something is valuable—a feeling that cannot be guaranteed by any existing rule—and the social recognition to confirm, at least temporarily, this feeling.

As has been mentioned, however, such judgements should not be seen as limited to the sphere of beauty, as we might mistakenly assume by reading Kant, or the sphere of finance, as we might mistakenly assume by reading Keynes. Instead, and through the atmospheres of information facilitated by ambient media, such aesthetic judgements—ungrounded decisions that nevertheless require general assent by way of an accepted norm—have become a common feature of life under neoliberal governance. Indeed, the proliferation of league tables and rankings for all manner of goods—healthcare, education, and, by way of the "likes" and "shares" of social media, even communication and self-expression—speaks to the ubiquity of such judgments in everyday life. Beyond this, and by drawing on the aesthetic theory of Sianne Ngai, we can argue that a specific aesthetic judgement has become, not only more common alongside the rise of neoliberalism and ambient media, but is also inextricably connected to the ethical injunctions that have emerged in response to QAnon and conspiracy theory. For Ngai, "the interesting" is one of the most understudied and yet important contemporary aesthetic categories. Gaining prominence as a category of aesthetic judgement through the work of late eighteenth and early nineteenth century German romantic literary critics, *interesting*, as a term applied to literary art, was connected to a "moment marked by a radically expanded and accelerated circulation of printed media and the emergence of a bourgeois public sphere, by an unprecedented explosion of new literary genres" (Ngai 2012, 120–121). For example, Ngai points to Friedrich Schlegel's 1797 text *On the Study of Greek Poetry*, in which modern poetry, and "the whole aesthetic development [*Bildung*] of modernity" is characterised in terms of an orientation towards the interesting, and away from the universal (Schlegel 2001, 35; 252). As Schelgel states in the provocative opening of this text, "it is obvious that *modern poetry* either *has not yet attained the goal towards which it is striving*, or that its striving has no established goal, its development [*Bildung*] no specific direction, the sum of its history no regular continuity, the whole no unity" (Schlegel 2001, 17; 217). As Ngai explains, this lack of direction or clearly established goal associates the interesting with "a specific temporality [...] that of the interminable or perpetually ongoing" (Ngai 2012, 121).

Given this temporality, for Ngai the hesitant or wavering quality of the interesting as a category of aesthetic judgement is key to understanding its underlying structure. As Ngai writes, the function of the interesting as an aesthetic judgement seems to be that of "ascribing value to that which seems to differ, in a yet-to-be-conceptualised way, from a general expectation or norm whose exact concept may itself be missing at the moment of judgement" (Ngai 2012, 112). Put differently, the description of a phenomenon as interesting could be taken as the assertion that the phenomenon in question has an as of yet unclear value, and that this value might reveal itself with further discussion or inquiry. To declare something is interesting is certainly not to describe it in terms of the harmony and perfection associated with the aesthetic category of beauty, or the awe and terror of the sublime, but, instead, to characterise it in terms of the experience of "a calm, if not necessarily weak, affective intensity whose minimalism is somehow understood to secure its link to ratiocinative cognition and to facilitate the formation of social ties" (Ngai 2012, 112–113). Or, as Ngai states further:

> when I am compelled to make public my appraisal of something as interesting, I am speaking precisely from my conviction that it is objectively worth paying attention to and appraising, regardless of my appraisal's vulnerability to time. When we judge, say, a bad movie to be interesting (and when we say interesting, we often do mean "bad but nonetheless interesting"), we are therefore essentially making a plea for extending the period of the act of aesthetic evaluation: let us keep on talking about this movie; let us continue giving it attention even though it is not particularly good.
> (Ngai 2012, 170)

Far from being a category of aesthetic judgement limited to the sphere of art, Ngai's account of the interesting arguably describes the logic that underpins what I have called ethics of examination without commitments. Put differently, the aforementioned expectation that one stays informed and connected sees the subject of ambient media provided with the injunction to limit themselves to the aesthetic sphere of the interesting. Faced with an abundance of competing narratives, facts, traditions, and rules—or, to use a perhaps unfashionable turn of phrase, given a general "incredulity towards metanarratives" (Lyotard 1984, xxiv)—to encounter the world as harmonious and perfect—that is to say, beautiful—would seem quaint and naïve, the product, perhaps, of inability to comprehend the world's complexity. Similarly, to take pleasure in the world as overwhelming and unrepresentable—that is to say, sublime—could be viewed as irresponsible, the product, perhaps, of an over-eagerness that betrays our collective duty to wait with interest to see what future research and results will show. I would argue, then, that what Ngai describes under the auspices of the interesting fleshes out the perhaps unintended ethical injunction provided by books like *When Bad Thinking Happens to Good People*. Against the supposed recklessness of those who surf the impact zones of the digital sublime, an ethics of examination that makes enquiries into the self and world without unshakable prior commitments to politics, ethics, or economic incentives—or a metaphysical notion of truth—could be understood as an interesting ethical imperative.

Contested Enchantments

How then should we assess QAnon's purported resonance, and its ethical rejoinder in the form of the push-pull of the interesting's commitment to temporal and evaluative affirmation and distanciation? One could assert, in support of Rosa, that this ethical project of examination without commitments—as I have unpacked through Ngai's aesthetic logic of the interesting—is further proof of the general culture of mute calculation that structures modernity, impedes resonance, and threatens to exacerbate alienation. In the face of the pseudo-resonance offered by ambient media, and embodied in the example of QAnon, Rosa might contend that we need *true resonance* and not further subordination of resonance to rationality, methodology, and logic. As we have shown, there are good reasons to view QAnon as an ambient media "echo chamber," insofar as its adherents can become gripped by an unwavering certainty that reduces the world and the other to the status of something to be manipulated, and often violently so.

Although I want to be careful not to suggest any false equivalences, it is useful to compare the philosopher Rob Sips's reflections on his own psychotic episodes and the experiences of re-enchantment associated with QAnon in order to elaborate this point. Sips explains that his first psychotic episode began with a radical change in perspective, although not in terms of delusions and hallucinations, but in terms of his "world as a meaningful whole" (2019, 952). What Sips appears to be saying is that, through the onset of his psychosis the very presupposed interpretative frame that structured his experience of things and people shifted radically. This might differ from the lay-conception of what psychosis entails, since, on Sips' account, his existing perspective on the world was not interrupted by hallucinatory things or people, but, instead, the very interpretive framework used to make sense of things and people changed. As he writes, "important to understand, I believe, is that psychosis affects this pre-reflective framework that makes the world appear as familiar, stable, and trusted" (2019, 952). Sips centres this shift in perspective around what he calls the "aha-experience," a sudden flash of insight through which fundamental truths about reality are revealed (2019, 953). As Sips puts it:

> during psychosis, I could suddenly notice things that had never grabbed my attention before. I perceived the world anew as if awaking from a dogmatic slumber. In part, this implies a realization and seeing of complexity in things that we normally take for granted, which makes one literally question everything.
>
> (2019, 953)

Although drawing on distinct intellectual traditions, this discussion of the "aha-experience" shows clear parallels with Jodi Dean's Lacanian theorisation of conspiracy theory. For Dean, the conspiracy theorist and the psychotic share an affectively charged experience characterised by a strong feeling that "everything is meaningful by virtue of pointing to something else" (2009, 150). As Bruce Fink has argued, the psychotic experience is differentiated in Lacanian discourse from other symptomatic structures—such as neurosis— by an overwhelming certainty and lack of doubt (1999, 84). In a manner comparable to Sips, Fink downplays hallucination in his overview of Lacanian theorisation of psychosis, insofar as the psychotic most likely knows that others do not see or experience what the psychotic encounters. Regardless of whether or not the psychotic understands that what they are experiencing is inaccessible to others, that it is "not part of a socially shared reality," they are, according to Fink, convinced that "he or she has been *chosen* among all others to hear or see it, or it concerns only him or her" (1999, 84). Rather than being plagued by fantasy the psychotic is plagued by meaning: "the psychotic is convinced not necessarily of the 'reality' of what he or she sees or hears, but of the fact that it means something, and that this meaning involves him or her" (1999, 84). We can argue that the QAnon adherent faces a similar problem. Unlike the experience of the interesting, where a kind of ethical and libidinal connection is established with doubt, the sublime experience of the world's complexity and inherent meaning is both what re-enchants and what alienates. As Sips has argued, the aha-experience should be dialectically related to what he calls the anti-aha-experience, in that, "while the aha-experience connects and reorients, the anti-aha-experience shatters into pieces and is literally and figuratively a disorienting experience" (2019, 953). As such, both the conspiracy theorist and the psychotic must navigate a certainty and an experience of connectivity that can alienate those who have doubts, and the experience of such certainty dissolving into a sense of painful fragmentation:

> in contrast to the positive feeling that accompanies the aha-experience, the anti-aha-experience is shocking, terrifying, utterly destructive, disorienting, painful, and difficult to understand or to explain to others.
>
> (2019, 954)

Following such a discussion, and, again, without drawing any false synonymity, it is possible that many QAnon adherents, especially the most violent ones, do not hold resonant relationships to the world. Indeed, insofar as such certainty reduces the other—whether the other person or thing, the world, or the self as other—to a caricature that cannot speak in its own voice, and must thereby be manipulated, one can mount the argument that such experiences do not fit Rosa's theory of resonance. However, even if we adhere to this interpretation of Rosa's theory, isn't it hasty to suppose that all QAnon adherents exhibit this kind of conviction or certainty? Research on conspirituality would seem to suggest that this is the case. As Zeeuw and Gekker write, "whereas classical accounts of conspiracy theories typically assume that users hold these theories to be true, this assumption cannot be transferred to online spaces like 4chan" (2023, 2). While there is much writing dedicated to QAnon's beginnings as an inside joke or troll, Zeeuw and Gekker are pointing at a deeper ambiguity. The question is not merely, to what extent was or even is QAnon a self-conscious game, but, beyond this, to what extent can belief and its disclosure be distinguished? "To what extent do people engaging with QAnon content actually believe in it, or do they instead play at believing?" wonder Zeeuw and Gekker, only to pose the further question, "do these oppositions still hold in a post-truth public sphere where attention has seemingly become the only relevant metric and engagement is king?" (2023, 2). Indeed, drawing on the work of the anthropologist Giovanna Parmigiani, we can view QAnon's adherents as perhaps engaging in the what she calls "conspiracy-believing" as opposed to "belief in conspiracies" (2021).

Following Parmigiani's work, we can argue that a conventional limitation of research into conspiracy theory communities is the emphasis on representational accounts of these aforementioned theories. Put differently, the conventional understanding of conspiracy theories holds that a claim such as "9/11 was an inside job" is meant to have the same epistemological status as a statement like "World War 2 ended in 1945." Presumably, the latter statement is made without concern for whether an interlocutor would agree that it is true—the speaker would simply hold that it is true, and if the interlocutor did not agree they would simply be mistaken. This kind of representational account of truth—where a statement is intended to refer to an external reality independent of either the speaker or the interlocutor—aligns with what Parmigiani calls "belief in conspiracies," and while Parmigiani seems well aware of the fact that such statements are made within conspiracy theory communities, she nevertheless maintains that an emphasis on this kind of statement can distract us from the prevalence of "conspiracy-believing." As such, Parmigiani's work suggests that a statement like "9/11 was an inside job" should be understood as an aesthetic judgement, and one that is intended to foster intersubjective agreement. As she writes, "as a practice, *conspiracy-believing* […] is not primarily a cognitive enterprise; rather, it is an affective, sensory, aesthetic, 'participatory' one" (2021, 519). As Kant argued, while an aesthetic judgement like "x is beautiful" does not necessitate agreement, since there is no pre-existing rule either party can appeal to in order to adjudicate correctness, it is nevertheless inseparable from the sense that the interlocutor *ought* to agree. Similarly, the truth content of a conspiracy theory—such as the theory that key members of the Bush administration orchestrated the terrorist attack on the Twin Towers—cannot be determined through an appeal to a pre-existing rule—indeed, were the conspiracy theory to coincide with the conventional account of events it would function as a mere restatement of conventional wisdom. As Parmigiani states, her research into communities of conspiracy-belief suggested that:

> the validation of a conspiracy theory […] does not come mainly from the logic of its internal argument nor by the 'academic reliability' aura that surrounds it. Rather, it comes from the fact that it is adopted and accepted by a wide community of *especially sensible* people, "people who reason along the same lines," as my Pagan friend put it.
> (2021, 521)

Such an account offers, not only the possibility of radically redescribing QAnon adherents such that many, but certainly not all, of their lore and conspiracy theory can be understood as aesthetic judgements underpinned by the logic of the interesting articulated by Ngai, but also the possibility of rethinking the ethics of the interesting as, not always, but occasionally, a minor mode of resonance. Following Parmigiani, QAnon lore can be read as interesting insofar as it facilitates intersubjective dialogue that gestures towards an indeterminate temporality. Put differently, QAnon as ambient culture can be read as interesting because of its speculative quality, that is to say, its capacity to engage participants in dialogue that suggests, but does not guarantee, that the validity or truthfulness of its statements might be revealed at a future time: "so let's keep talking." In this way, QAnon lore can be seen as irreducible to either the mute detachment of the neoliberal ideal—the cautious calculations of *homo economicus*—or the sublime experience of ecstatic truth and certainty. By the same token, we can rethink the ethics of examination without commitment as involving a weak or minor form of resonance, insofar as, to return to Ngai's theory of the interesting, examination requires "a calm, if not necessarily weak, affective intensity" in order to spur it outward (2012, 113). Rather than reducing the interesting to a defence against ambient media's atmospheres of information—although, as I have tried to show, it certainly can function in this way—we can also view it as a cautious and weak mode of resonance, a fragile mode of opening oneself up to the other's voice, albeit while maintaining that the other's message is ultimately futural. In this way, the interesting could be read as similar to the ethics and politics of weakness and vulnerability discussed by Roquet, Hagood, and LaBelle in the previous chapter, despite the fact that it is unlikely such figures would recognise such an ethics or politics emanating from QAnon and its adherents.

Where then does this leave us with regards to the question of the relationship between resonance, environmental illness, and ambient media? What I have attempted to show in this chapter is the ambiguity of resonance and alienation as Rosa has developed them. I have pursued this by framing QAnon—a potential use of ambient media to respond to what are commonly referred to as "mental illnesses"—in such a way as to lead to two possible responses. Firstly, one could concede that QAnon does exhibit resonance so long as its adherents maintain an ethics of the interesting rather than being drawn into the digital sublime. When QAnon is merely an aesthetic game that provides individuals and communities with a sense that the world is open and enchanted, even if only minimally, then it can be viewed as offering resonance. However, once a QAnon adherent moves beyond the aesthetic experience of the interesting and is gripped by the pleasure and paranoia of the digital sublime, such that they become certain that the other is to become an object of manipulation, resonance has now arguably fallen into pseudo-resonance, if not alienation. Secondly, one could argue that QAnon cannot be viewed as a source of resonance due to the content of its lore being reprehensible, whether this is defined in moral or epistemological terms. If we approach QAnon in terms of the second response, then we would have to admit that a theory of resonance is incomplete without a more clearly articulated normative content, thereby undermining resonance as articulated by Rosa—and, furthermore, raising the question of how we are to know which beliefs and behaviours are alienated and which are resonant. If we approach QAnon in terms of the first response, however, we seem to be similarly stuck with the problem, not only of who gets to decide what behaviours or beliefs constitute the dangerous certainty of the digital sublime, and which exhibit the openness of the ethics of the interesting, but also whether an experience of the digital sublime pertains to any sense of conviction, or whether it is itself merely one interesting experience among others. Regardless of the path taken, if we can acknowledge that QAnon exhibits potential for resonance and alienation, albeit in an undecidable way, we find ourselves burdened with ethical, political, and conceptual problems that have plagued the study of "mental illness" for centuries—that is, short of whether or not *they* fit in with *us*, how are we to decide the status of alienation? And, further, who gets to decide which modes of existence are enchanted or disenchanted?

Notes

1. Regarding the latter, Sommer notes that "QAnon grew so big that it split into two factions: 'J-Anon' and the QArmyJapanFlynn,' a group with a special devotion to former Trump national security adviser Michael Flynn" (2023, 197).
2. For example, while *Mulholland Drive* (Lynch 2001) and *L.A. Confidential* (Hanson 1997) are both neo-noir films set in Los Angeles that focus, among other things, on the darker aspects of the Hollywood and the entertainment industry, *Mulholland Drive* has a much cooler plot, in that the lack of clear narrative affords—although certainly does not guarantee—greater room for the audience to interpret what the characters are experiencing and what the film is ultimately trying to say.
3. Again, while the violence perpetrated by QAnon's adherents should not be downplayed, it is important to note that many of the most distributing themes within QAnon share a continuity with more ubiquitous aspects of Anglo-American culture. For example, and as a theorist like Lee Edelman would likely remind us, the "save the children" fixations of QAnon—fixations which often see marginalised people, and especially Queer and Trans people, targeted for harassment and abuse—surely cannot be extricated from the broader uses of the figure of the child, by both conservative and liberal factions, to mobilise all manner of revanchist political projects (See: Edelman 2004).
4. While I don't have the space to unpack it here, Vogl's argument is not that media and technology should be viewed as ultimately underpinned by financial power. Instead, Vogl's project is to show the coevolution of contemporary media and financial power, one that has resulted in novel forms of subjectivity and governance.

References

Bennett, Jane. 2001. *The Enchantments of Modern Life: Attachments, Crossings, and Ethics*. Princeton: Princeton University Press.
Berkowitz, Reed. 2021. "QAnon Resembles the Games I Design: But for Believes, There Is No Winning". *The Washington Post*, 11 May. https://www.washingtonpost.com/outlook/qanon-game-plays-believers/2021/05/10/31d8ea46-928b-11eb-a74e-1f4cf89fd948_story.html
Bloom, Mia, and Moskalenko, Sophia. 2021. *Pastels and Pedophiles: Inside the Mind of QAnon*. Stanford: Stanford University Press.
Bruns, Axel. 2008. *Blogs, Wikipedia, Second Life and Beyond: From Production to Produsage*. New York: Peter Lang.
Davies, Will. 2018. *Nervous States: How Feelings Took Over the World*. London: Vintage.
Davies, Hugh. 2022. "The Gamification of Conspiracy: QAnon as Alternate Reality Game". *Acta Ludologica* 5.1: 60–79.
Dean, Jodi. 2009. *Democracy and Other Neoliberal Fantasies: Communicative Capitalism and Left Politics*. Durham: Duke University Press.
Demuru, Paolo. 2022. "Qanons, Anti-vaxxers, and Alternative Health Influencers: A Cultural Semiotic Perspective on the Links Between Conspiracy Theories,

Spirituality, and Wellness During the Covid-19 Pandemic". *Social Semiotics* 32.5: 588–605.
Dickinson, Tim. 2021. "How the Anti-Vaxxers Got Red-Pilled". *Rolling Stone*, 10 February. https://www.rollingstone.com/culture/culture-features/qanon-anti-vax-covid-vaccine-conspiracy-theory-1125197/
Edelman, Lee. 2004. *No Future: Queer Theory and the Death Drive*. Durham: Duke University Press.
Fink, Bruce. 1999. *A Clinical Introduction to Lacanian Psychoanalysis: Theory and Technique*. Cambridge: Harvard University Press.
Frankel, Eddy. 2021. "QAnon: The Italian Artists Who May Have Inspired America's Most Dangerous Conspiracy Theory". *The Art Newspaper*, 19 January. https://www.theartnewspaper.com/2021/01/19/qanon-the-italian-artists-who-may-have-inspired-americas-most-dangerous-conspiracy-theory
Haiven, Max, et al. 2022. "Interview with Wu Ming 1: QAnon, Collective Creativity, and the (Ab)uses of Enchantment". *Theory, Culture & Society* 39.7–8: 253–268.
Hanson, Curtis, director. *L.A. Confidential*. Warner Bros, 1997. 2hr, 18 min.
Icke, David. 2014. *The Perception Deception*. London: David Icke Books.
Jameson, Fredric. 2009. *The Cultural Turn: Selected Writings on the Postmodern, 1983–1998*. London: Verso.
Jensen, Michael, and Kane, Sheehan. 2021. "QAnon Offenders in the United States". *NC-START*. https://www.start.umd.edu/publication/qanonoffenders-united-states
Kant, Immanuel. 1987. *The Critique of Judgement*. Trans. Werner S. Pluhar. Indianapolis: Hackett.
Keynes, John Maynard. 1993. *The General Theory of Employment, Interest, and Money*. London: The Macmillan Press.
Latour, Bruno. 1993. *We Have Never Been Modern*. Trans. Catherine Porter. Cambridge: Harvard University Press.
Lynch, David, director. Mulholland Drive. Studio Canal, 2001. 2hr, 27 min.
Lyotard, Jean-François. 1984. *The Postmodern Condition: A Report on Knowledge*. Trans. Geoff Bennington and Brian Massumi. Minneapolis: University of Minnesota Press.
Mazzarella, William. 2017. *The Mana of Mass Society*. Chicago: University of Chicago Press.
McCarraher, Eugene. 2019. *The Enchantments of Mammon: How Capitalism Became the Religion of Modernity*. Cambridge: Harvard University Press.
McLuhan, Marshall. 1994. *Understanding Media: The Extensions of Man*. Cambridge: MIT Press.
Meltzer, Marisa. 2021. "QAnon's Unexpected Roots in New Age Spirituality". *The Washington Post*, 29 March. https://www.washingtonpost.com/magazine/2021/03/29/qanon-new-age-spirituality/
Nadler, Steven, and Shapiro, Lawrence. 2021. *When Bad Thinking Happens to Good People: How Philosophy Can Save Us From Ourselves*. Princeton: Princeton University Press.
Ngai, Sianne. 2012. *Our Aesthetic Categories: Zany, Cute, Interesting*. Cambridge: Harvard University Press.
Parmigiani, Giovanna. 2021. "Magic and Politics: Conspirituality and COVID-19". *Journal of the American Academy of Religion* 89.2: 506–529.

Rosa, Hartmut. 2019. *Resonance: A Sociology of Our Relationship to the World*. Trans. James Wagner. Oxford: Polity Press.
Rosenfeld, Sophia. 2011. *Common Sense: A Political History*. Cambridge: Harvard University Press.
Schlegel, Friedrich. 2001. *On the Study of Greek Poetry*. Trans. Stuart Barnett. New York: State University of New York Press.
Sips, Rob. 2019. "Psychosis as a Dialectic of Aha- and Anti-Aha-Experiences". *Schizophrenia Bulletin* 45.5: 952–955.
Smith, Nicholas. 2022. "A Quasi-Fideist Approach to QAnon". *Social Epistemology: A Journal of Knowledge, Culture and Policy* 36.3: 360–377.
Sommer, Will. 2023. *Trust the Plan: The Rise of QAnon and the Conspiracy That Unhinged America*. New York: Harper Collins.
Taylor, Charles. 2007. *A Secular Age*. Cambridge: Harvard University Press.
Ward, Charlotte, and Voas, David. 2011. "The Emergence of Conspirituality". *Journal of Contemporary Religion* 26.1: 103–121.
Weber, Max. 2002. *The Protestant Ethic and the Spirit of Capitalism*. Trans. Peter Baehr and Gordon C. Wells. London: Penguin.
Wendling, Mike. 2021. "QAnon: What Is It and Where Did It Come From?" *BBC*, 6 January. https://www.bbc.com/news/53498434
Wiseman, Eva. 2021. "The dark side of wellness: the overlap between spiritual thinking and far-right conspiracies" *The Guardian*, 17 October. https://www.theguardian.com/lifeandstyle/2021/oct/17/eva-wiseman-conspirituality-the-dark-side-of-wellness-how-it-all-got-so-toxic
Vogl, Joseph. 2022. *Capital and Ressentiment: A Short Theory of the Present*. Trans. Neil Solomon. London: Polity.
Zeeuw, Daniël de, and Gekker, Alex. 2023. "A God-Tier LARP? QAnon as Conspiracy Fictioning". *Social Media + Society* 9.1: 1–14.

Conclusion

Across a variety of institutions and media, the last few decades have seen increased concerns around the expansion of the notions of "mental illness," and an overflowing of psychiatric knowledge beyond its institutional confines, such that some have begun to raise the alarm over our supposed collective inability to keep separate those thoughts and behaviours that relate to the pathological or to the healthy and normal. For example, in the view of psychiatrist and co-architect of the DSM-IV Allen Frances, we should be concerned that the very concept of normality is under attack from profiteering pharmaceutical companies and a therapeutic culture that sees "mental illness" underpinning even the most ubiquitous forms of everyday unhappiness and strife (2014). As I have shown throughout this book, academics and journalists have scrutinised the rampant rates of self-diagnosis and the potential misuse of psychiatric knowledge that purportedly results from the dominance of ambient media platforms like TikTok, YouTube, and Twitter. Rather than viewing this expansion of psychiatric categories beyond their conventional borders as either a symptom of specific online platforms or a symptom of the profit incentives of specific industries, in this book I have attempted to approach this culture of diagnosis as being, at least in part, a product of an ambient cultural condition—a condition that arises both from specific technologies and from discourse of relationality that others have associated with the emergence of a denaturalised ecological paradigm (Hörl 2017). As I have attempted to show, by paying closer attention to the ways ambient media co-constitute new modes of attention, intimacy, and health, we can better consider what is emerging out of the now declining biologistic paradigm of "mental health." This has been done in the hope of revealing that, increasingly, being "mentally healthy" means being seen (by oneself and others) to be exhibiting resonance in the manner described by Rosa. Not only will individuals be expected to maintain open and transformative relationships with themselves and with others, but they will also be expected to maintain such relationships with the non-human world—and the latter is not limited to what is conventionally understood as "nature," but will also include the digital technologies that track, record, and audit us.

Conclusion 103

Accordingly, this book has been preoccupied with the question of how to critically appraise this ecological logic of interrelation that underpins contemporary media and environmental illness. I have attempted to articulate that there are good reasons to be optimistic about some aspects of this ambient and relational logic, insofar as it assists in returning the individual to their world, resists both biological and sociological modes of reductionism, and assists in an expansive and non-normative notion of what "mental health" could be. Despite key differences in the level of their concern regarding ambient media, and its potential to trap the individual within the simulacrum of connection to the other, my reading of Rosa, Roquet, Hagood, Labelle, and Flore, has attempted to show a broad agreement within much contemporary social and media theory around the need to embrace what is radical about an expansive notion of relationality, and to move beyond the mute instrumentality, and the strong egoism of bourgeois subjectivity. Such perspectives have a great deal of value for critical discussions around "mental healthcare," especially since they resist locating the "problem" within the individual's mind or brain, or within a limited field of relationality that restricts itself to romantic relationships or the bourgeois family.

For some theorists, however, such a reliance on the figure of the bourgeois individual misses the extent to which what I have been calling ambient subjectivity has already become, if not hegemonic, then at least worthy of much greater critical scrutiny. This is a point made compellingly by Rey Chow, who argues that contemporary critics of digital technology—and here she is specifically referring to Byung-Chul Han and Giorgio Agamben, but one could make a similar challenge to the aforementioned theorists in this book—display an "unwitting reliance on the older (phenomenological) associations of the *bourgeois* subject—one who has a considerable attention span and a capacity for emotional depth and who is capable of being gripped by or of losing herself in aesthetic experience" (2021, 160). Following Chow, one could argue that the task for critical thought today is no longer to worry about the hermetic escape of the self into itself via ambient media—the individual's absorption into narcissistic alienation or media echo chambers *a la* Roquet's strong self or Rosa's mute individualist. Instead, the problem is perhaps less that of interiority—regardless of whether one espouses a "conservative" politics of reclaiming interiority or a "progressive" politics of further relinquishing it—and more one of relationality and openness, or, even, ambience. As Chow puts it:

> how do we come to terms with a kind of self that, instead of being rife and torn with inner antagonisms (as in the case of the confessing Christian sinner or psychotherapy patient), is habituated to ephemeral images, voices, sounds, emails, and text messages coming at it incessantly from "ambient screens" big and small?
>
> (Chow 2021, 160)

Whether one cautiously embraces the ambient subject as opening up a path beyond the alienation of bourgeois subjectivity or maintains that such subjectivity only exists in the nostalgic tracts of social and media theorists, the logic of ambient relationality that I have been discussing is all too often characterised in terms of an image of uninterrupted expansion, connection, and dispersion. In the discourses both of those who lament the disappearance of bourgeois interiority and of those who embrace the ambient self's connection to what is other is a shared marginalising of the ambivalences and antagonisms that produce and emerge through a general and denaturalised ecology of relations. As Eva Giraud writes, albeit in reference to the dominance of "entanglement" within the contemporary humanities, "rather than focus on an ethics based on relationality and entanglement"—a theoretical gesture that will be all too common to most readers—"it is important to more fully flesh out an ethics of exclusion, which pays attention to the entities, practices, and ways of being that are *foreclosed* when other entangled realities are materialized" (Giraud 2019, 2).

Similarly, this book has attempted to think through, not only the well-established reality that what I have been calling environmental illness can be precipitated and exacerbated by ambient media's capacity to encourage the fantasy of a self-reliant and self-absorbed individual, but also the possibility that relationality—and even those forms of relationality that meet Rosa's standards for resonance—can produce alienation and suffering. As such, this book has tried to draw attention to the ambivalences and ambiguities that persist, not only through the internal rifts and double binds of the self-regulating neoliberal subject, but also through the ecological and dispersed relationality of ambient media and ambient subjectivity. If, as this book suggests, the painful inner world of "mental illness" is truly being reconceptualised in terms of the open and shared experience of environmental illness, we should be under no illusions of the promise of a general diminishment of pain. Moreover, this book has tried to show the risks of obscuring such pain by framing it as a side effect of our collective inability to embrace the right kind of relationality—whether it is understood in terms of resonance, weakness, vulnerability, or empathy. As the example of QAnon reveals, we should be open to resonance's undecidable relationship with environmental illness and ambient media, such that we are aware of the potentially ceaseless task of responding to the pain, or perhaps even alienation, produced *through* resonance. As such, we should affirm the non-normative version of Rosa's social theory, such that environmental illness can be embraced as a means of avoiding biologically and sociologically reductive accounts of existential pain, and creating space for thinking through the connection between self and other, human and non-human, and the organic and inorganic in the production of environmental illness. In other words, if we can accept that ambient media and the notion of environmental illness reveal the world's interconnectedness as both the condition for existential suffering and its overcoming, we can attempt to embrace a pluralistic account of suffering—one that is open to the truly heterogenous forms pain and its care can take—without establishing a specific notion of relationality, even a highly formalistic one like Rosa's, *as a principle for determining what makes life worth living.*

If we can avoid turning relationality—and especially the open and transformative relationality of resonance—into a principle that we must adhere to in our attempts to conceptualise environmental illness and its therapies, we should also be open to what is potentially lost or excluded, to return to Giraud's point, in the becoming ambient of "mental healthcare." To take just one example, the psychoanalytic clinic is potentially threatened by the contemporary embrace of ambient media and the expansion of ecological logics of self. As stated in the first chapter, the psychoanalytic clinic—with its fixed location, dyadic therapeutic structure, and sense of enclosure—could seem distinctly out of sync with the ambient and ambulatory character of digital applications and wearables, which have helped to produce a world in which "a schizophrenic out for a walk is a better model than a neurotic lying on an analyst's couch" (Deleuze and Guattari 2009, 2). Moreover, the analyst--analysand relation seems to lack the logic of produsage that underpins those ambiently mediated cultural responses to contemporary alienation—and especially loneliness—such as QAnon. It would be tempting to defend the psychoanalytic clinic on the grounds that it offers an important experience of interiority—away from the surveillance capitalism of ubiquitous digital media—or that it offers a sense of structured, if not hierarchical, dialogue that is so often missing in the dispersed conversations offered by ambient media, and especially social media. However, I would contend that this would be an analytic mistake, and one that is unlikely to endear many to the plight of the psychoanalytic session. Instead of discussing the psychoanalytic session as being opposed to the ambient logics discussed in this book, we should, as was foreshadowed in the first chapter, attempt to understand psychoanalysis—at least in its Freudio–Lacanian form—as offering ambient logics, especially of attention and intimacy, that are irreducible to those offered by ambient digital media.

For example, in his history of the techniques and technologies of recumbent thought, Nathan Kravis highlights the analyst's couch as a "locus of both intimacy *and* distancing" insofar as the couch directs the analysand's gaze away from the analyst, and, at least potentially, assists in opening up the analysand to free association—with their speech indirectly directed at the analyst who is positioned out of view (2017, 161). In what appears like a blend of muteness and resonance, the couch allows the analysand the "transgressive potential" of opening their speech beyond what is conventionally shareable, through the "neutrality, abstinence, and anonymity" of a specific technique of distanciation (Kravis 2017, 161). As such, the analytic session could be seen as a forerunner to many of the ambient media case studies presented in this book—the indirect communication of the ambient room, the attention to

Conclusion

marginal sounds found in ASMR, and the mixing of potentially disconnected elements as found in QAnon, for example. And yet, given that the psychoanalytic session cannot entail the massified relationality of most of the ambient media discussed—because of its dyadic structure, but also because of its cost—and because it cannot provide the individual with the 24/7 accessibility of Woebot or an international QAnon community, it is nevertheless at risk of being maligned as outdated and conservative.

My closing argument is not that the psychoanalytic session is superior to the forms of ambient therapy discussed within this book, nor is it to suggest that the ecological and pluralistic notion of environmental illness should be replaced by the perhaps more delimited structures of Lacanian analysis—such as those of the psychotic or the neurotic. Instead, this book has attempted to problematise the affirmation of relationality as a principle of emancipation and, through such a problematisation, to open up the question, not of how we can escape the straightjackets of ambient media or the mute self, but of the unavoidable ambivalences that we must contend with now that a logic of escape has come to underpin almost all aspects of life. As stated at the beginning of this book, "a breath of fresh air, a relationship with the outside world" (Deleuze and Guattari 2009, 2); today this statement could just as easily refer to the experience of environmental illness as to its treatment.

References

Chow, Rey. 2021. *A Face Drawn in the Sand: Humanistic Inquiry and Foucault in the Present*. New York: Columbia University Press.
Deleuze, Gilles, and Guattari, Félix. 2009. *Anti-Oedipus: Capitalism and Schizophrenia*. Trans. Robert Hurley and Helen R. Lane. London: Penguin.
Frances, Allen. 2014. *Saving Normal: An Insider's Revolt Against Out-of-Control Psychiatric Diagnosis, DSM-5, Big Pharma, and the Medicalization of Ordinary Life*. New York: Harper Collins.
Giraud, Eva H. 2019. *What Comes After Entanglement? Activism, Anthropocentrism, and an Ethics of Exclusion*. Durham: Duke University Press.
Hörl, Erich. 2017. "Introduction to General Ecology: The Ecologization of Thinking". In *General Ecology: The New Ecological Paradigm*. Eds. Erich Hörl with James Burton. London: Bloomsbury. 1–76.
Kravis, Nathan. 2017. *On the Couch: A Repressed History of the Analytic Couch from Plato to Freud*. Cambridge: MIT Press.

Index

Agamben, Giorgio 103
alienation 8, 34, 37–41, 44–47, 50, 52, 55–58, 61, 66–67, 73–75, 79, 83, 94, 98–99, 103–105; and Althusser, Louis 37–38; as disenchantment 78–79
ambient media: and affective curation 47–48, 51, 56–61, 65; ambient intimacy 17, 19, 21–23, 28, 49, 61–62, 66, 80, 102, 105; ambient music 6, 56–57, 59, 62–63; ambient room 16; ambient screens 14–16; headphones 47–48, 63; as orphic media 60–61; Roquet's definition of 58; and self-regulation 48, 59; smartphone 3, 6, 16, 19–20, 47–49, 51, 64, 79, 81; wearables 11, 16, 19–20, 51–52, 62, 105
ambient therapeutic media: Abilify MyCite 61, 64–65; alternate reality game 83–84; ASMR 61–64, 106; Chatbot therapists 21, 48–50, 106; ecological momentary intervention 19–20

Benjamin, Walter 17–19, 22, 29, 58, 91
biopolitics 12, 58

Chamayou, Grégoire 24
Chow, Rey 103
conspirituality 81–82, 96–97
COVID-19 1–3, 6, 79–80, 82–83, 88
Csíkszentmihályi, Mihály 67–74; flow 67–69, 72–73

Deleuze, Gilles 11, 23, 26, 30, 105–106

ecology: denaturalised ecology 1, 55, 102, 104; general ecology 75, 104
Ehrenberg, Alain 24–25
enchantment 78, 85–86, 94
Eno, Brian 6, 56–57, 59, 62–63
entanglement 34, 64–65, 69, 81, 104
environmental illness 3, 5, 7–8, 11, 14, 27–29, 33–34, 40, 44, 52, 55, 65, 74–75, 78, 83, 98, 103–106
environmentalization/ environmentality 26
Eric Hörl 1–2, 5, 7, 9, 17, 26–28, 30, 40, 102, 106

fascism 74
Flore, Jacinthe 64–66
Foucault, Michel 2, 24, 26–27, 38, 67
Freud, Sigmund 21–23, 70, 91, 105

gamification 22
Guattari, Félix 11, 23, 26, 30, 105–106

Han, Byung-Chul 51, 103

Icke, David 80–82
Insel, Thomas 12
Instagram 43, 52

Jaeggi, Rahel 38–39
Jameson, Fredric 90

Kant, Immanuel 86, 90–92, 97
Keynes, John Maynard 90–92

Lacanian analysis 95, 105–106; enjoyment 70, 72, 74

mad studies 4–5
mental illness: anorexia nervosa 41–44, 53–54; anxiety 1, 3, 6, 8, 21, 26, 32, 45, 49, 51, 53, 55, 58–60, 62, 67–70, 72, 76–77, 81; depression 1, 3, 5–6, 21, 29–31, 40–41, 44, 51, 54–55, 62, 71, 81; as ecological 1–2; under erasure (*sous rature*) 5; as neuroecosocial 13; neuroreductionist view of 13; schizophrenia (psychosis) 1, 5–6, 11–12, 20–21, 30, 64, 94–96, 101, 105–106

neoliberalism 5, 8, 12, 23–24, 26–28, 41, 44, 47–51, 56–59, 61, 66–67, 83, 89, 92, 97, 104
new materialism 33–34
Ngai, Sianne 92–94, 97–98
Nietzsche, Friedrich 70–71, 73–74, 77

QAnon 75, 79–89, 92, 94–98, 104–106

Reckwitz, Andreas 25–26
resonance 7–8, 22, 29, 34–41, 44–47, 49–52, 55–56, 58, 61, 63, 66–67, 69, 73–76, 78–79, 81, 83, 87, 94, 96–98, 102, 104–105; pseudo-resonance 47, 50, 55, 66, 83, 94, 98; resonance and the non-human 45–47, 50; Rosa on resonance and technology 43, 49–52, 66; Rosa's definition 35–36
Rosa, Hartmut 3, 7–8, 29, 34–53, 55–59, 61, 66–67, 69, 73–75, 78–79, 83, 87, 94, 96, 98, 102–105
Rose, Nikolas 13, 24

Skinner, B.F. 26
Spotify 48

Thiel, Peter 90, 92
TikTok 3, 8–10, 52, 89, 102
Trump, Donald 75, 79–80, 82, 84
Twitter 52, 102

vulnerability 51–61, 65, 68, 69

Weber, Max 66–67, 69–70, 78
Wu Ming/Luther Blisset 84–87

Zupančič, Alenka 70–74, 77